The Lament of the Single Practitioner

The

Essays on the Law

Lament

Mordecai Rosenfeld

of the

Foreword by Louis Auchincloss

Single

The University of Georgia Press

Practitioner

Athens and London

© 1988 by the University of Georgia Press
Athens, Georgia 30602
Foreword to *The Lament of the Single Practitioner:*
Essays on the Law © 1988 by Louis Auchincloss
All rights reserved
Designed by Richard Hendel
Set in Walbaum

The paper in this book meets the guidelines for permanence
and durability of the Committee on Production Guidelines
for Book Longevity of the Council on Library Resources.

Printed in the United States of America
92 91 90 89 88   5 4 3 2 1

Library of Congress Cataloging in Publication Data

Rosenfeld, Mordecai.
     The lament of the single practitioner: essays on the law /
Mordecai Rosenfeld; foreword by Louis Auchincloss.
          p.   cm.
     Originally appeared in the New York law journal.
     ISBN 0-8203-1066-2 (alk. paper)
     1. Law—United States—Anecdotes.   I. Title.
K184.R67 1988
349.73—dc19
[347.3]   88-17515
                                                             CIP

British Library Cataloging in Publication Data available

The author and the publisher wish to thank the *New York Law
Journal* for their kind permission to reprint these essays,
all of which first appeared in the *Journal*.

To Susan, on our twenty-fifth anniversary

Contents

Foreword

J ustice Oliver Wendell Holmes once characterized freedom of speech as "the right of a fool to drool." For all its dry pungency there is a note of contemptuous elitism in the definition that would not suit Mordecai Rosenfeld in the least. For he can find as many fools in the courts and congresses that claim the glory of guarding our liberty of expression as among the thoughtless speechifyers who have little to say that seems to merit protection. Indeed, no one is safe from his probing wit. In these columns you will find Holmes in 1910 agreeing with Justice White's dissenting (thank God) opinion that shackling a convict is not a cruel and inhuman punishment "since while the chain may be irksome it is evidently not intended to prevent the performance of the penalty of hard labor." And Rosenfeld deems even the almost sacrosanct Learned Hand "panicking" in an opinion where that great liberal jurist finds the rantings of the American Communist party, that feeble and petulant shard of a larger conspiracy, a "clear and present danger" to the American colossus.

Rosenfeld refers to his family's origin in Vilna, Lithuania, where I once attended a writers' conference. I recall that going to Vilna from Moscow was like passing from a murky basement to an attic solarium. From Slav gloom we escaped to welcoming smiles. No doubt Rosenfeld owes to the country of his family's origin some of the good spirit that irradiates these essays, drowning pomposity and bureaucracy and even man's inhumanity to man in waves of devastating laughter.

But there is also comfort and even inspiration in the deep, solid, cleansing common sense of this classically educated, widely read legal philosopher and single practitioner at the New York bar. Why should we be impressed, he wants to know, by gigantic corporate law firms that have everything in the world in their chambers but poetry, by legislatures that are drowned in the small print of their endless enactments, by bureaucrats who strangle their own ends in their fetish of means?

It sometimes seems that modern society cannot offer enough examples of absurdity to fill these joyous columns: a constitutional amendment to make English the official language with only English (?) words permitted in official documents; Judge Scalia's proposal that the federal courts should be forums for the big (?) cases only; the sanction of state laws allowing schools to ban books "in poor taste"; the barring from the mails of pamphlets on venereal disease and family planning; Attorney General Meese's suggestion that only the named parties are bound by a Supreme Court decision; New York's making it a felony to wear a bullet-proof vest while illegally using a firearm. And he has this to say of John Shad's gift of $30 million to Harvard Business School to improve Wall Street ethics: "I've seen those Harvard Business School types in action, and believe me, $30 million won't make a dent."

But sometimes he is downright mad, as with the book *Postmortem* that attempted to prove that Sacco and Vanzetti had received a fairer trial than generally supposed. Here there is no place for laughter—only a grimly effective summary of the principal outrages permitted in court by Judge Thayer.

My favorite is the essay "The Quality of Mercy," where Rosenfeld comments on the decision in *Rummel v. Estelle,* where the Supreme Court upheld in March 1980, 5–4, a life sentence imposed in Texas on a man who was convicted of a third felony. His three crimes, all nonviolent money frauds, involved a total sum of $229.11. The dissent was a learned retelling of the long history of human rights in England and this country. Rosenfeld said that the majority should have said only this: "It is unconscionable, hence unconstitutional, to send Mr. Rummel to jail for life because this is the United States of America."

Louis Auchincloss

An Introduction: The Four-Minute Mile

When I began to write these pieces in 1979, I changed my fantasies. Before then I had fantasized about the four-minute mile.

Running the four-minute mile had been a vague goal since my Brooklyn childhood, when I raced the Ocean Avenue trolley car from Avenue J to Avenue I, a very long block that included my own apartment building (1439 Ocean Avenue, Brooklyn, New York, no zips then), the New York Telephone Company building, and a Protestant church. I also raced the Pilgrim Laundry electric delivery truck over the same course every Thursday afternoon. I would win only if the trolley (or truck) was slowed by traffic and if my sidewalk route was clear. The motormen would often greet me by clanging their bell, especially as they increased their lead toward the end.

Until Dr. Roger Bannister actually did it, I thought that I had a chance to be the first. My high school had no track team, but I did run for my college, albeit as a sprinter. I thought that my speed and determination just might make me the famous one. I couldn't complain when Bannister beat me to it, because I had never run a competitive race longer than the quarter-mile, and that only on the relay team; the 220 was my preferred distance. After Bannister, to whom I bore no grudge, I had to reorient my thoughts. I began to think how much easier life would be if I, instead of that Englishman, had been the first to break the magic barrier. For instance, when I had trouble finding a job after graduating from law school, I mused how easy it would be had I been the one to have won the historic race. And that told me something about the law: who you were was more important than what you were. But that was no secret to most people.

I was surprised, at the beginning of practice, at just how grim the law was. Judges are grim (their black frocks are most appropriate), lawyers are grim, and clients are grim. The subject matter of lawsuits always involves something unhappy—someone reneged on a promise or took unfair advantage or hated his (or her) spouse or was inattentive (except to the ballgame) while cruising down the highway. I knew from the start that the law was not for me.

But alternatives were hard to conjure up. I had once considered teaching at a law school, but I was told in my early years that I did not have enough experience; and I was told later, when my experience was extensive, that law faculties resented lawyers who had become expert through a mercenary practice. Anyway, I was disqualified because I had not been a turner-outer of articles in unreadable legalese. But if being a teacher required me to write about the law I was determined to be defiant and to write in English, my native tongue. I considered that I had an unusual perspective on the law, being a single practitioner and having litigated on my own many important cases (largely in the corporate law and securities law areas). I thought that I understood better than most how the law and lawyers operated.

In 1979 I was asked to participate in a seminar being organized by the *New York Law Journal* to discuss the topic of expert witnesses. About fifty young lawyers had signed up to listen and to take notes; I was the last of the panelists scheduled to speak. By late afternoon, when my turn was approaching, I noticed a drowsiness among the audience. I decided to forgo my prepared text and to wing it with a lighter touch. I asserted that an expert was just an academic who wanted to earn some fees, and that there was not a proposition in the world for which some expert, somewhere, could not be found. For instance, I noted that Son of Sam's defense was insanity; he acknowledged that he had murdered or maimed a half-dozen young women, all with long brown hair, but claimed that he did so only because he had followed the commands of his neighbor's dog. Although he might have been the craziest defendant ever, New York State was, nonetheless, able to find two expert psychiatrists who testified that Son of Sam was sane. Those experts explained that he was sane because there is really no such thing as "normal" or "abnormal"; rather (they concluded) "we all have our quirks." There was great laughter, and when the audience filled out the opinion forms, I received the most praise. The *Law Journal* then asked if I would do other seminars, but I responded that I would prefer to write the pieces down. I've written about one essay a month for the *Law Journal* since, all done casually with no deadlines.

The object of most legal writing is to score points the way the Chicago Bears score points, by the force of brute size. The object of these pieces is the opposite, to make all points crisply, and sometimes laughingly. And the subject of these essays is the obvious one—that the mysterious, majestic, mighty law, the law that radiates from the mountaintops of Olympus and Sinai, is not always well served by those who operate the winches of the law. Too often judges, lawyers, clerks, and chaired professors seem to spend every working hour straining to move the law one notch to accommodate this or that narrow interest.

It has all been done blatantly, because subtlety is not among the law's characteristics. And the critics who have berated the law for its most obvious flaws have been equally heavy-handed. Law bashing, however, changes nothing. If you rail at the law it rails back. The law excels in those exchanges of heavy artillery and, as at the battle of Belleau Wood, no one wins. But if you laugh at the law, poke at it, sometimes even ridicule it, the law has no answer; as a result you might even convince someone else. Of course, changing a few minds about the law is not the same as actually changing the law itself, but it is a start. Unlike the laws of nature, our earthbound laws are not immutable, and that's the wonderful, the exciting part. We may not ever be able to exceed the speed of light (which really ought not matter, because the speed of light is fast enough even for the trains on the Tokyo-Osaka run), but the laws that govern man-to-man can always be made better, like the records in track and field that are made to be broken.

My perspective of the legal system and legal warfare is colored, I know, by the fact that I have always been a single practitioner litigating against law firms with division strength. I have had to rely on the quick thrust; my adversaries always prefer trench warfare. When I began writing these essays they were, philosophically and emotionally, an extension of my one-man practice, one person trying to change things in a very small way, one person trying to be heard. As with the trolleys I used to race, winning isn't as important as making a statement, an individual, stubborn, one-man statement.

The Lament of the Single Practitioner

I. *Some Personal Experiences*

Mom Should Have Been a Senator

Mom should have been a United States senator. When I was a boy in Brooklyn, all the children would gather every steamy summer evening in front of the Telephone Building, which was recessed enough so that the boys could play stickball and the girls hop-scotch on the sidewalk. It was a time before air-conditioning, and there was no relief from summer anywhere. Every evening, after supper, Mom would issue the same instruction: "Mordecai, you can go out and play, but don't perspire."

Mom should have been a senator because she, too, thought she could enforce her personal preferences and whims by fiat. With similar faith, Senator Helms has introduced a bill (S. 158) "To provide that human life shall be deemed to exist from conception," and Senator Denton has introduced a bill (S. 1090) "To promote self-discipline and chastity" among the nation's adolescents (defined at Section 1902[5] as an individual under the age of nineteen; the bill is aimed only at the unwed).

The purpose of this essay is not to discuss the merits of those bills but only the power to enact them. There are two limits on Congress: nature and the Constitution. In physics, nothing can be colder than absolute zero. Congress could not, by passing a law, simply add another ice cube (perhaps to satisfy an ice-cube– producing state like Alaska) and, thereby, lower the temperature by even one degree. The formal constitutional limit is contained at Article I, section 8, which sets forth the only areas of congressional competence (e.g., to lay and collect taxes, to raise and support armies, to establish post offices). The bills proposed by Senators Helms and Denton may exceed both limits on Congress's power.

If you want to know when life began before Senator Helms all you need do is tiptoe through any graveyard and read the dates there written in stone. But philosophically speaking, it is always harder to know when things began than when they ended. Did the spaceship *Columbia* begin when the jet engine was developed in the 1950s, or with the Wright Brothers or when Daedalus and

Icarus exited from Crete? When Icarus exceeded his limits and flew too close to the sun, he crashed; maybe there is a lesson there for the Senate. And did World War II begin when Germany invaded Poland in September 1939 or at Versailles in 1919 or when the walls of Jericho came tumbling down? The more you think about some things, the earlier they seem to have begun.

If something as mysterious as life doesn't begin at birth, Senator Helms may be taking too short a view if he goes back only a few months to conception. A better argument can be made that each life began twenty billion years ago, even before there was a United States Senate. The question of when life begins involves two profound philosophical inquiries: What is life? and What is meant by "begins"? It is unconventional for the answers to be given by a majority vote of a hundred dam-trading politicians, some of whom have not studied Schopenhauer in years.

Debate on Senator Denton's chastity bill has turned out to be somewhat different. While some question whether the Congress, which just gave us Abscam, is the very best group to decide morality, the logicians all favor S. 1090. Their legal reasoning is this: the bill seeks to prevent promiscuity only among adolescents (under nineteen years). Under familiar legislative exegesis, everything not specifically discouraged is, thereby, endorsed. (In Latin: *Expressio unius est exclusio alterius*). Therefore, argue all the Aristotelians, Senator Denton's bill necessarily favors adult (over nineteen years) promiscuity. Not that the Washington after-hours crowd needs a law, but some legal scholars are even arguing that nubile adults who demur might be guilty of a misdemeanor. There is a reason why the Founding Fathers limited Congress to building post offices and fixing import duties.

If Mom were in the Senate, there would be at least two new bills introduced in the personal, limitless spirit of S. 158 and S. 1090: a bill "To Require Everyone to Wear a Sweater When Mom Was Cold"; and a bill "To Require Everyone to Like Rhubarb." The rhubarb bill may require some legislative history. When I was a boy in Brooklyn, Mom frequently made rhubarb for dessert. I did not like rhubarb, and so stated. Whereupon Mom would say that it tasted like strawberry ice cream, to which my response was "Then let's have strawberry ice cream." To which Mom retorted that she had made it a new way and that I should try it; but I refused.

Mom seemed very hurt and repeated that she had used a brand new recipe that took hours, and at the very least I should sample it. Under that kind of pressure, I ate some rhubarb but reported again that I didn't like it. The matter was dropped for about a week, when Mom again made rhubarb for dessert. I said, "Mom, I don't like rhubarb." To which she answered, "But you ate it last week."

That's why Mom should have been a senator. Or at least a federal judge.

July 9, 1981

The Lament of the Single Practitioner

The United States, winding up its case against IBM, has asked that IBM produce an additional five billion pages of documents; IBM has complained that it will take 62,000 man-years to comply. Is there a place in corporate litigation for the single practitioner?

Perhaps by getting to the office early and by skipping dessert it could be done in 57,000 years. And if there were a crash program to expedite the task—using loafers instead of shoes (saving tying and untying time every day) and by ignoring all secular and religious holidays (Heaven forfend)—the documents might be assembled in 42,500 years, give or take a fortnight. Any further speed-up would cause genuine hardship.

But upon reflection, perhaps no case should be beyond the limits of a single practitioner, because all cases, even those with five billion *additional* pages of documents, must be decided by a single practitioner—his Honor, the judge. And few judges will skip dessert or ignore a holiday. How does a judge decide a case where there are billions and billions of pages of countervailing arguments? The same way easy cases are decided, by sortilege.

Although some would think that enormous law firms have grown up in response to enormous cases, the sequence is quite the other way around. Cases that could be managed quite well by one person, or two, are converted into pantagruelian litigations when processed by what is known as a Big Firm. A Big Firm has hundreds and hundreds of lawyers whose thinking is organized around the Word Processing Center; the basic machine in the center is a computer linked to a law library. The largest firm in the country, based in Chicago, has over five hundred lawyers and branch offices in twenty-four cities on four continents; rather than a law firm, it appears to be a soccer league.

Big Firms, like the armies they emulate, have three or four support troops for every frontline lawyer. There are secretaries, librarians, messengers, chefs, waitresses, bartenders, masseurs, 6 Xerox operators, computer operators, accountants, nurses, and office managers. But among those in the front lines or those in the rear staging areas there are no poets.

When a case is referred to the office, the single practitioner has no choice but to think upon it. The Big Firm, however, begins by referring the matter to the Word Processing Center. This is how it works: A client has driven his saffron-striped mauve Lamborghini through a red light and has received a ticket. The first question referred to the firm's computer would be, Is it against the law to drive through a red light? The computer, within two minutes, will respond with a print-out of all the statutes in the world (arranged alphabetically by continent) that deal with red traffic lights and the legal consequence of not stopping when they shine. When the senior partner analyzes the junior partner's evaluation of the statutory complexities, he might send down for more specific information: "Are there any cases in the English-speaking world that involve a saffron-striped mauve Lamborghini?" If the computer whirs and concludes that there are no such cases, the Big Firm might then advise its client that the legality of his ticket appears to be a case of first impression and if challenged the outcome would be in doubt. And so a mighty litigation is begun.

The use of the computer saves valuable man-hours, so that lawyers can be used where they are really needed, in court. A Big Firm, aware that its clients must always be well represented, will dispatch a phalanx to court even if the matter is routine. A phalanx consists of one senior partner, two middle partners, three junior partners, four associates, and five paralegals, who carry an index to the entire file and whisper to the associates, who whisper to the junior partners, and so on up the line in response to a question that began with the senior partner and traveled swiftly down the chain of command.

A Litigation Team consists of two phalanxes. One of the most embarrassing things that can happen to a Big Firm is to appear in court underrepresented; that is, to have fewer lawyers present than the Opposition. To deal with that emergency, each Big Firm has specially trained commando phalanxes that are on constant alert and can be airlifted to any courtroom in the country on ten minutes' notice. Eternal vigilance is the price of freedom.

The Big Firm is as unwieldy as the dinosaur. When you think

about it, there are very few things that five hundred people can do better than one thoughtful person. It was one person who proved Newton wrong and who reshaped the way we understand the laws of nature. Poems, plays, and symphonies are written by one person. Even if all the Word Processing Centers of all the Big Firms were linked into one giant grid, they could not write one couplet. Or know what is just.

Bar associations and judges, always concerned with the spiraling cost of interminable litigation, call conferences periodically to deal with the problem. At each conference each Big Firm is represented by one senior partner, two middle partners, three younger partners, four associates, five paralegals, and a partridge in a pear tree. As they bemoan their increasing overhead, they hire more and more lawyers underfoot.

The Big Firm mirrors some of our national characteristics. We love skyscrapers, the taller the better; we love airplanes that carry hundreds of people and a grand piano; we prefer to watch a TV program that fifty million others are watching. Is a law case something that hundreds can participate in? Is it like a tug-of-war with dozens of lawyers and paralegals on each side, where he who wins has the most pull? Is law like a chess game, where he who wins is the most insightful? But perhaps the law is not a contest. Perhaps the law is more serene, like a poem reflecting sensitivity in every rhyme and every meter. Yes, that's it; the law is like a poem; but among the hundreds of persons who work in a Big Firm none is a poet. Walt Whitman and William O. Douglas saw America the same way; and Chief Justice Warren and Langston Hughes. Perhaps the majesty of the law is more clearly described by the words "Beauty is truth, truth beauty" than all the piles and piles of five billion pages of documents being sorted and catalogued by hundreds of faceless lawyers.

October 5, 1979

Hold That Line!

A recent news item in the *Law Journal* reported that several of the big firms, the standard-setters, had decided "to hold the line at $43,500" for beginning lawyers. When I began to practice law, the line my employers held was a tauter one. I began at $65 a week; I had asked for $70.

The pay then was not only poorer, but the work was much harder. There was no Xerox-Savin-3M-Pitney Bowes-IBM photostat machine, so that much of my day was spent in the bar association library, painstakingly copying relevant quotes by longhand. It must have also been before the invention of the ballpoint pen, because I still remember that my right thumb and left-side shirt pockets were permanently stained blue-black. Most days, from about ten in the morning until lunch time, I would hunt for the relevant cases; after lunch, I'd begin the tedious copying process. I soon began to dislike, then detest, windy judges. I rated Chief Justice John Marshall and Justice Felix Frankfurter as the wordiest. Justice Douglas was most to the point. Justice Cardozo strove the hardest to be literary, but oh! how he became mired in aimless purple passages.

My handwriting had always been poor, and sometimes I couldn't read my own notes, especially those written in the late afternoon. So while the typist would leave a few spaces or a line blank, I'd race back to the bar association, reread the case, and write the quote more legibly. Since I didn't ever want my trip to be a mere wasted duplication, especially if it was raining, I'd usually also add a few new sentences to my quote.

As I became more experienced, I began to spend less time in locating the critical authorities than in copying them (a punctilious process that could not be speeded). One had to justify such a perverse use of time, and I sometimes romanticized that what I was doing was in the ancient tradition of my People; for was I not just like a Torah scribe of ancient Vilna, copying each letter of the law faithfully?

Writing by hand, and for a low wage, was not only part of the Mosaic culture; it was part of the heritage of the common law as well. It has been recounted how Abraham Lincoln once walked several miles to a very rich client's home (the roads were out), drew his will (which he wrote by hand), and then charged a fee of $5. For legal services to the County of Menard, which included ten separate court appearances, lawyer Lincoln billed $20. His rate for arguing a case before the Illinois Supreme Court was usually between $5 and $10. In order to stop price-cutting (it was before the bite of the antitrust laws) the Chicago Bar Association in 1852 adopted a minimum-fee schedule: Legal advice was $2, drafting a pleading was $1, and a trial in court of record would cost $10. How today's clients must romanticize about the good ol' days.

The biggest difference between those days and now is not the Xerox machine, not even the one that churns out thousands of copies a second, collates them, staples them, and walks them to the post office, pre-bundled by zip code. Nor the memory typewriter that makes every old brief a new one at the touch of a button. The biggest difference, rather, is the Big Firm, that assemblage of several hundred lawyers who hardly know each other but who huddle together for warmth and comfort under one letterhead. They are the ones who, without any discernible increase in a beginner's ability, have raised their once modest pay to these astronomical heights. The Big Firms now pay a callow youth as much as some great law schools pay their full professors; and more than many states pay their judges.

Here's one psychological explanation: it's the way that the Big Boys assert themselves. It's rather ego-building to pay an entry-level clerk $43,500. And if that innocent lad or lassie is paid $43,500, junior partners need a few hundred thousand dollars, as up the dizzying scale one goes. And now even the Biggest of the Big are beginning to balk, because salaries for legal freshmen are at a level that George Steinbrenner reserves for certain ballplayers, superstars and duds.

Late in the fourth quarter of the Chicago Bears-Washington Redskin National Football League championship game (1940), the 'Skins defense suddenly stiffened, and the chant "Hold That Line!" resounded in Griffith Stadium. But there, as here, it was a bit late; the score was already 73–0.

October 26, 1982

11

———

Some
Personal
Experiences

Guilt by (Bar) Association

The local press recently carried the triumphant story of how the USS *Iowa* Surface Action Group will be stationed in Stapleton, Staten Island, bringing thousands of jobs that almost went, instead, to Boston or Newport. I was in Stapleton once myself. May the navy use it for target practice.

After I had passed the bar examination, I received a detailed but seemingly harmless questionnaire from the bar association Ethics Committee. I was required to list every job I had ever held and every organization I had ever belonged to. I was not a joiner and replied immediately. A few weeks later I received a routine letter advising that I would be interviewed by a bar association examiner whose office was in Stapleton, Staten Island.

I had never been to, or heard of, Stapleton before. As I rode the Avenue J bus to the ferry terminal, I began to review in my mind all my youthful misdeeds, for the Brooklyn Bar Association was famous for its attention to the smallest indiscretion.

The one incident that began to trouble me was a semiofficial act that had taken place many years before, during a blackout in 1942 or 1943. When the air-raid sirens sounded, my father, who was an air-raid warden, ran into the street wearing his official hard hat, emblazoned "CD" for Civil Defense. I was a youthful, hatless messenger, and it was my assignment to report to a basement office in case I had to bicycle with a highly secret (and perhaps coded) message to the neighboring air-raid warden site; I also delivered coffee.

When the sirens sounded at night, the main job of the wardens was to make sure that all lights were out in our apartment building. We all knew that the Luftwaffe's main war goal was to bomb the vital military crossroad of Ocean Avenue and Avenue J (Brooklyn), and we were determined that they would not be guided to their destination by any stray light. Once, as I was rushing to the subterranean messenger office, I saw candlelight flicker from apartment 5F. Without thinking, I yelled with patriotic zeal,

"Mrs. Polansky, blow it out." The all-clear sounded without any Messerschmitts having reached Brooklyn, and I returned to finish my homework. Mom was very critical: "Mordecai, Mrs. Polansky is older than you. The war is no excuse for bad manners. You should have said 'Please.' Go upstairs and apologize."

There followed a long discussion, popular in those years, of whether the ends ever justified the means; but I refused to go on the less philosophical ground that old Mrs. Polansky was probably asleep. The Polanskys owned the kosher delicatessen on Avenue J, and Mom bought a year's supply of corned beef by way of apologizing. It was, until edged out by the Marshall Plan several years later, the largest war-wrought indemnification in history. As the Avenue J bus rumbled toward the ferry, I became increasingly worried about the interview and wished that I had yelled "Please" to Mrs. Polansky.

The examiner did not say "Hello" and did not shake my offered hand. Rather, he informed me directly that two of my questionnaire answers were matters of serious concern. First, he was disturbed about my membership in Students for Democratic Action. I explained that the Brown Chapter had been founded in my senior year by Mrs. Eleanor Roosevelt, who had personally urged all students to involve themselves politically. I also noted that both the New York governor (Harriman) and mayor (Wagner) were members of Americans for Democratic Action, SDA's parent group. The examiner replied that since he would approve neither the governor nor the mayor—nor Mrs. Roosevelt, he added—for admission to the bar, it would be inconsistent to approve me.

His second serious doubt was caused by my brief membership in the Legal Aid Society while at Yale Law School. I explained, by way of defense, that the dean himself had posted a notice requesting that all students with a few free hours help in a project being sponsored by the New Haven Public Defender's Office. They were asking law students to interview selected persons who had been arrested but not tried, to see if there were extenuating circumstances that would support a dismissal of charges. The person I had interviewed had come to America as an infant and was threatened with deportation to Poland for a rather minor, nonviolent, foolish crime. I had recommended leniency. The examiner then rendered his opinion: I had practiced law without a license and hence was ineligible for admission to the bar.

I left the examiner's office trembling. It sounds terribly treacly now, but when the ferry back to Brooklyn passed in sight of the Statue of Liberty I suddenly put everything in a different perspective. I thought of how my grandparents had passed this very spot over fifty years before, full of hope. And here I was, a graduate of Brown and Yale and about to become a lawyer. The main difference, I thought, of having reached the statue's protection was that anti-Semitic examiners (for I always assumed that was the problem) did not always prevail, as they had in Vilna.

And I was, indeed, admitted to the bar right on schedule, as were all the other Stapleton rejectees; the full bar association Ethics Committee rejected each of the examiner's several negative reports and even apologized. But beyond those immediate happy results, how could the bar association have permitted that ogre to terrorize a group of young law graduates every year? I've been distrustful of all bar associations ever since. And I've always been a little ashamed of my own weakness. I was so relieved to be admitted to the bar on time and so fearful of jeopardizing job opportunities that I never, until this essay, complained. I should have yelled loudly and most impolitely. Even Mom would have approved.

September 16, 1983

The Rosenfeld Years

I saw a news item that former President Carter had hurried back to Plains, Georgia, to complete his memoirs, tentatively named *The Carter Years*. That prompted me to complete this essay, because book stores have only so much shelf space for the reminiscences of former public servants, and I, too, once worked for the United States government. I was, during the Eisenhower administration, a trial attorney with the Mail Rates Division of the Civil Aeronautics Board; my rank was GS-11, rather low on the bureaucratic scale.

I did not have to endure round-the-clock Secret Service protection, because I remember calculating that approximately 825,000 government employees in Washington, D.C., alone would have to retire or be disqualified before I would, under the then prevailing laws of succession, become the president.

Although I had been tentatively hired by the operations branch, I still needed what was euphemistically called "administrative clearance." It seems that the Republicans had been out of office for so long that they wanted control even over the lowly GS-11 positions. Although it violated the letter and spirit of the Civil Service Act, discreet inquiry was made of my political affiliation. I had been advised of the problem (I was a Democrat) and parried the question by stating that my family had voted both ways. I was satisfied in my own mind that I was being truthful because my paternal grandmother, who had liked his looks and his historical middle name, had voted for Warren Gamaliel Harding.

My parents were upset because they thought that working in Mail Rates meant that I was sorting letters and canceling stamps, which they said would be fine with them if I really liked it but that I was probably overqualified in light of my law degree from Yale. But the term "Mail Rates" was just another of those government semantic subterfuges. Mail Rates was the device through which Uncle Sam subsidized the air carriers. If an airline was certified to carry the mail it was, ipso facto, entitled to a subsidy even if it didn't carry one post card. The rates formula involved many elements, most of which were surprisingly subjective. So Milt Shapiro (the section chief), Henry Switkay (his deputy), Tom Chew, Steve Gelband, Jack Padrick (for a short while), and I sat around and divided $72 million (more or less) a year among thirteen so-called local service carriers; local service airlines linked places like Peoria and Dubuque with small cities.

I was just a Brooklyn boy, and to me $72 million a year was a heady amount to allocate. But the airline recipients always wanted more and argued that we were pikers because the Maritime Commission, just across Constitution Avenue, doled out each and every fiscal year subsidies of $4 billion or $5 billion. Whether they hoodwinked the public too, and called it "Sea Mail Rates," I never did find out.

The airline lawyers did make some strained arguments to increase their clients' share. In order to qualify for a Mail Rates subsidy a certificated airline had to have an operating loss (which was easy to incur on the Peoria, Dubuque, etc., runs); the government made up the difference, and paid them a profit, too. Therefore, we had to examine all their expenses to determine whether (and the extent to which) those expenses would be "recognized" (that is, recompensed by the CAB).

My first administrative suggestion was to limit the salary that the Board would pay to the president of an airline to the salary that was then being paid to the president of the United States. I argued that it was wrong for the United States to pay a higher salary to the president of Pacific-California Coastal Airways (for instance) than it paid to the man who ran the whole Western Alliance. The airline lawyers vigorously disagreed, arguing that nothing in the world was harder than keeping schedules in foggy weather. Since the airlines operated in just about every state of the Union, they had unusual strength in the Congress. With prodding from the Hill, a compromise was worked out which paid the presidents of the several airlines more than the president of the Republic, but only slightly.

The most dramatic lesson in *realpolitik* that I ever learned involved a long litigation called the *Capital Gains* case. The airlines frequently sold their older airplanes at a great profit (that is, for a capital gain), and the Board would automatically deduct that profit from the subsidy payments. The Board's logic was impeccable: the subsidy was a government handout, and if you made money by selling an old DC-3 your subsidy need was thereby reduced. The airlines resisted because, of course, they wanted both their subsidy and their capital gains.

After a long litigation, which ended in the Supreme Court, the Board prevailed. We had quite a nice party over at Mail Rates, because the airlines had been represented by the most prestigious of the Wall Street law firms. But the very day the Supreme Court's decision was announced, the airlines' man in Congress introduced a new law that said: "When computing airlines' subsidies, capital gains shall not be taken into account." Faster than the Concorde, that bill was enacted and signed into law. If there was an ironic twist, it was that we had to help draft the final wording of that law, for we were, in the legal sense, mere arms of the Congress. The drafting was very dutifully done.

The best part of working at the CAB was the camaraderie. I hope that I'm not sentimentalizing the past. Tom Chew was from Garrett, Indiana, and was always being kidded about it: "How's the Garrett Symphony?" "When's the Garrett baseball team going to join the majors?" Tom would respond by telling us of the many intrigues of Garrett life, some of which he necessarily inflated. To check up, I once sent a $5 bill to the Garrett newspaper, for which I received about ten recent issues. I took one to the office, and while everyone else was reading the *Wall Street Journal,* I put my feet up on my desk and ostentatiously read the *Garrett Bugle* (or was it the *Herald?*). Tom was amazed, but I read on casually as if I read it every day. "Where did you get that?" I replied that I had bought it in the local out-of-town newspaper stand. At lunchtime Tom went there to buy a few copies, full of pride that the *Bugle* (or *Herald*) was up there with the *New York Times,* the *Baltimore Sun,* and the *St. Louis Post-Dispatch.* He was mad at me for only a few minutes but had to be more careful thereafter about his description of high-stepping in Garrett.

One of the saddest things about deregulation, other than the fact that airplanes are now probably flying all over the heavens helter-skelter in every direction, is that the CAB will soon disappear. I learned more about the real world in my three years there than I have learned in all the years since.

And now Mr. Carter and I are both writing our recollections. He and I both worked in Washington, we both worked in the government, and we have now returned to our respective native cities to reflect. We both handed out a lot of good money to good people and we both have daughters named Amy. If there is any difference between us, it is that I probably got along better with the Congress.

December 23, 1983

The Law as Minor League

I was not allowed to play baseball until I had finished my homework, because if I didn't finish my homework I would not get into college, and if I didn't graduate from college I couldn't go to law school. I was then almost seven. No one could have foretold, in those ancient days, that baseball would do more for justice than all the lawyers, judges, law professors, and Law Day speeches put together. This essay is prompted by a recent book about baseball immortal Jackie Robinson (*Baseball's Great Experiment*, by Jules Tygiel, Oxford University Press, 1983).

I bought the book for the nostalgic comfort of reading about Pee Wee, Dixie (I had not forgotten that he hit .357 in 1944), the Duke, Campy, and Red Barber. But as I continued to read, the book became too disquieting, too distressing. It is still hard to believe, although, of course, I know the fact very well, that blacks were not allowed to play in the majors until 1947.

Where, I kept thinking, was the law? And where were all those people who today link arms when a nuclear power plant is built, who try to switch on the sun instead? I began to brood that the law seemed to be the very last institution to recognize injustice, the caboose among professions.

The clergy, of course, was way ahead; Henry Ward Beecher was preaching his abolitionist sermons in Brooklyn's Plymouth Congregationalist Church (just a few blocks from where Jackie Robinson would make his major league debut in Ebbets Field) at the very moment that the Supreme Court was announcing its Dred Scott decision. Novelists like Dickens, reporters like Lincoln Steffens and Jacob Riis, poets like Whitman and Yevtushenko, cartoonists like Herblock, all those genius musicians from Basin Street, and now athletes like Robinson and Campanella—all, it seemed, had been more effective champions of justice than the law. I almost panicked as I tried to think of a profession, any profession, that was more laggard. I finally settled on dentistry, but I suspect that that was a personal pique more related to a recent bill than to the merits of the case.

As I focused on the law's silent hypocrisy, I began to wonder about myself, too. Jackie Robinson had no greater fan; but I, who have lived almost my entire life in New York, have never really *known* a black person.

Only once did I share a personal experience with a black, and that was as a troubled but passive witness, long ago. The Brown track team—I ran first leg on the freshman mile relay—had left Boston Garden after the Knights of Columbus Meet and took several taxicabs to South Station for the last train to Providence. The driver of the cab in which I rode amused himself, and he thought us, by telling crude, anti-black jokes.

Riding with us was Charlie Chambers, a black teammate. None of us knew what to do, and our only action was not to give a tip. I remember still how hard it was for me to talk to Charlie about it, either on the train ride back or later, as we warmed up together by jogging, then racing, around the wooden track that was set up on the outside, just beyond Marvel Gym.

Rooting so hard for Robinson and still not knowing even one black person was so easy, as I think about it now, because No. 42 was, despite his commanding physical presence, partly a symbol, an abstraction, to most of us. The law, too, has always excelled in abstractions; hard cases were something else. That is why the Constitution could exist so comfortably side-by-side with Satchel Paige and Josh Gibson, and later Jackie Robinson, playing in the Negro Leagues.

Robinson's success and popular acceptance was a large factor in the law's desegregation of schools, pools, and water fountains, and in the ending of antimiscegenation statutes. When Mom heard a radio report that Mississippi's antimiscegenation statute was being challenged in the Supreme Court she asked me (her son, the law student) what such an odd-named statute was. I explained that the Mississippi Legislature had once enacted a law forbidding Jews and Gentiles from intermarrying. Mom actually applauded: "I didn't know that people from down there were so concerned." She looked at me—I was then still single—and wondered out loud which would be the wiser family course, to campaign at once for a similar law in New York or simply to move to Biloxi.

As the news report continued, I had to acknowledge that I had overstated the case, that the law being challenged prohibited whites and blacks from intermarrying. Mom was positively irate: "Whom you marry—that's your business." She correctly predicted that the Mississippi statute would be declared unconstitutional. In seeing the world through its own dark sunglasses, baseball was no different from Mom, or the rest of us.

The law is so slow to change because people are so slow to change. I now argue, just as Mom once did (although Mom had greater success), that the children should finish their homework before they go out to play.

January 23, 1984

Jingle Bells and the Supreme Court

S ince I already knew the result from the news media, I began to read *Lynch v. Donnelly* stoically, and with the dispassion of a Las Vegas bookmaker. What were the odds, I thought, that there existed five people in the whole world who thought that the Nativity scene was secular; and how staggering the odds must be that if there were five such people, they would all be judges sitting on the same court at the same time. Then I read this reference, tossed off so casually by Chief Justice Burger: "To forbid the use of this one passive symbol—the crèche—at the very time people were taking note of the season with Christmas hymns and carols in public schools . . . would be a stilted over-reaction contrary to our history." That brought back some sad memories.

Just after every Thanksgiving, the Christmas singing would begin at P.S. 152 (Brooklyn). It would start during Friday assembly with such neutral airs as *Jingle Bells* and *The Skaters Waltz*. But as December rolled on, the singing would spread to every classroom, and the repertory would expand to include such sacred pieces as *Ave Maria* and *Silent Night*. And just after every Thanksgiving—how I fretted over it—my father would give me a letter to deliver to the principal, suggesting that Christmas carols were out of place in a public school, and advising in no uncertain terms that I had been instructed not to sing them.

Every year I made a variety of arguments against delivering that fateful message. For instance, I had this practical point: I was a monotone and had what was considered to be the worst singing voice in Brooklyn. My position was that I would do "them" great damage if I were to join their chorus; I'd be a sort of flat, dissonant Benedict Arnold. I even promised to sing louder than usual, but that pitch failed. I followed with a rather philosophical point. My singing voice was so distracting that I was officially classified as a "listener," a "listener" being a person who mouthed the words but was asked, please, to make no sound. It was unnecessary, I urged, to send a letter announcing that I would not sing carols because the music teacher did not let me sing anything.

As I grew older and my debating skills sharpened, I made an argument that could be described as either Socratic (my definition, meaning it was a winner) or Talmudic (my father's, meaning it was a hair-splitter). There were, I noted, many Jewish musicians who played in the orchestra or sang in the chorus when, for instance, the New York Philharmonic performed Handel's *Messiah* or Bach's *Christmas Oratorio*. Did my father think that they should be excused? And if not, why should people with great musical talent be given some kind of religious dispensation, whereas the rules were strictly enforced against people with more humble ability; that, I said, was pure discrimination.

Nonetheless, every year the letter was dispatched. And every year, upon its receipt, the principal would read it and make the same comment: "Does that mean, Mordecai, that you won't be singing *Jingle Bells*?" I never responded but would turn very red and leave his office wishing for a fleeting moment that my grandparents had never left the warmth of the Vilna ghetto.

When it was graduation time, it was suggested to the faculty that I not be considered for valedictorian; my conduct, said the principal, had been disruptive. But the teachers' steadfast position was that my father's dispute with the administration had nothing to do with me. And so on graduation day I delivered the Valedictory, a memorized, condensed piece from *Reader's Digest*, written by the war correspondent Ernie Pyle.

I have always liked to excel, whether in sports or school. In that spirit, I have been rather proud that my singing voice was not just ordinarily bad but has always been regarded as among the very worst in the world. It is, therefore, with some sadness that I note that the Supreme Court in the *Lynch* case was more off-key than I've ever been.

April 5, 1984

Genesis, Chapter 22—A Respectful Dissent

The Bible and the Supreme Court of the United States are wrong, and Mr. and Mrs. Bernard Port of Houston, Texas, are right. The issue is the relationship of parent and child.

I have never understood why Abraham has been so lavishly praised for his willingness to sacrifice his innocent young son, Isaac. Although the Almighty blessed Abraham for his singular devotion ("I will multiply thy seed as the stars of heaven; . . . and thy seed shall possess the gate of his enemies"), I have always thought the Lord was only being polite. It was hard, even for Him, not to say something gracious to one willing to put his son upon the pyre. My own theory is that He was keenly disappointed and had hoped that Abraham would steadfastly refuse, for after all, Isaac was his own person and not Abraham's to give.

But whatever His private thoughts, the written law of Genesis 22 has for thousands of years given Bible-abiding fathers an awesome power. I, myself, was particularly aware of that because my dad was religious, as were my mother and brother; I, alone, was indifferent. There was, in my childhood, the weekly debate of whether I was required to attend Friday night and Saturday services; and even if not required, whether I should attend them just because I was living in my Father's house. I countered with: "Where am I supposed to live? I'm only nine years old."

In those years, the secular Friday night entertainment was "The Lone Ranger" and "Bill Stern's Sports Show," both radio events (TV was not yet). So the next debated question was, If I didn't go to services should I be allowed, instead, to listen to "junk" on the radio. I was almost always permitted to do so, provided I kept the volume down so that the neighbors would not know either of my dereliction or of my taste.

The next issue was Hebrew School. I was enrolled in an after-school, three-day-a-week program when I was six; all the others in my class were ten or eleven, preparing for their Bar Mitzvahs. I complained at home that I was out of my league, but the counterargument prevailed: Hebrew education should not be Bar Mitzvah-related, and if all the others were older it was only because they had started too late; they'd not make that mistake with me. And so it went, three times a week (Monday and Wednesday at 4 P.M., and Sunday morning).

When I was fifteen or sixteen, some ten years into my studies, I summoned up the courage to suggest that I switch to the once-a-week Sunday morning program. Being fifteen or sixteen years then was not like being fifteen or sixteen now; my allowance was thirty-five or forty cents a week, and the main right that I had was the right to be quiet. But I was determined to free up some afternoons, especially during the stickball and football (two-hand touch) seasons. Before I was allowed to switch I had to explain myself to the Hebrew School teachers, the principal, and the rabbi. You would think that I had decided to become a Methodist.

Liberation loomed, because I was admitted to Brown University, the first Midwood High School graduate so honored. But as soon as the acceptance arrived, Dad raised the matter of the college's kitchen not being kosher. He suggested that I live with an observant family in Providence, Rhode Island. I explained that since I did not intend to keep kosher after I had graduated from college I saw no point in abiding by those rules as an undergraduate. Upon my promise not to eat bacon, ham, other pork products, or shellfish (I did not know what shellfish was), the issue was dropped. I had four glorious years at college and even attended religious services now and then. I never wrote home about them; but then I rarely wrote home about anything.

The harsh law of Genesis 22, that a parent was required to sacrifice his (or her) child upon the command of a higher authority, persists to this day. One David Port of Houston, age seventeen, has been accused of murder. The Grand Jury subpoenaed his parents to give evidence against him. They refused, as who wouldn't, and were held in contempt. Their appeal reached the U.S. Supreme Court, but they have been (so far) turned down; the one justice (White) to whom the matter was referred refused to stay their jail sentence (*New York Times*, Sept. 29, p. 9). That is odd, because the law does not allow one spouse to testify against another even if he (or she) wants to. There are even cases of unlikely people (he a seventy-year-old gunslinger; she a twenty-year-old only witness without a dowry) marrying just for the purpose of invoking that privilege.

It is the law's ancient rule that nothing, not even sound evidence, may interfere with the sacred bonds of family. That rule should apply, and even more so, to the relationship of parent and child, but there seem to be no precedents, except this biblical one: the Book of Exodus (23:19) says, "Thou shalt not seethe a kid in his mother's milk."

Abraham was saved from slaying his son by a miracle. At the very last instant an angel from heaven called down: "Lay not thine hand upon the lad," and a substitute sacrificial ram appeared in a thicket. The Ports, too, need a touch of divine intervention now that the Supreme Court has refused to act. But I don't expect that they'll hear any gentle, saving voice from the he-man Texas sky.

October 30, 1984

The Law and Pete Reiser

Ronald Reagan, who has a job, favors lowering unemployment benefits. Some congressmen, whose positions are less secure, have urged an increase. While I myself am a liberal on that issue for personal reasons (soon to be set forth), I hope that the debate ends very soon. For each reference in the press to those unemployment payments is a painful reminder of the meanest day in my life.

It happened some twenty-five years ago, just before lunch, on the last Friday in June. One of the partners in the three-partner midtown law firm where I worked—it was my first job after law school, and I had been there some two and one-half years—called me to his office and with a studied casualness, told me that I was being discharged *that* day. For many months thereafter my only income was the government check.

My parents, who knew my compulsive diligence, were in greater shock than I. To lighten the atmosphere, I told them how really lucky I was. "True," I said, "I was fired without notice, without cause, and with practically no severance pay. But think how bad it would have been if my boss hadn't been a socialist." It got a small laugh and, I suspect, a few Republican votes in the next election.

And so once a week I would drive my old blue and gray Chevrolet to the local unemployment office, at East Thirteenth Street and Kings Highway in Brooklyn. As I drove, I thought of Will Rogers's remark, made to uplift spirits in the 1930s (and preserved on Edward R. Murrow's record, "I Can Hear It Now") that Americans were the only people in history who went to the poorhouse in an automobile (with the accent on the "mo").

At the unemployment office I would queue up with the rest of the out-of-work folks to have my book stamped by the clerk; it would be stamped only if you explained, as I always did successfully, that you had tried hard but futilely to find employment.

I began to recognize the same people each week, and some camaraderie developed. I was referred to as "the lawyer," not because I ever admitted to being one, but because I wore a shirt and

27

tie and jacket, even in August. People chatted as the line inched forward, about their lost jobs and struggling families. I listened and nodded but said very little, for I was really quite ashamed. Here was I, twenty-seven years old, in perfect health, a graduate of Brown University and Yale Law School, depending on the state for my support. I brooded that I was the first member of the family to have stood on a civilian government line since my grandparents had passed through Ellis Island.

To lift my sagging spirits I made a mental list of others who had been discarded but had made it. They were personal heroes. I thought of Pete Reiser, Dodger centerfielder, who had been sold by the St. Louis Cardinals for $100. In 1941, Pistol Pete hit .343 and led the league; he also led the Dodgers to the pennant. The Cardinals were second, two and one-half games behind; they would have won by a dozen had they not discarded Reiser, and that made me feel terrific. I thought, too, of how Abe Lincoln had lost the Illinois Senate race in 1858 but had come back strong.

The experience raised one question that I never have resolved: Could the law (which is noble) be separated from the practice of law (which is too often mean)? Were the two—the law and its practice—really one, like an object and its shape? Or were they more like music and its performance, for the Mozart sonata was always sublime, even if the violinist screeched. I didn't know the answer twenty-five years ago and I don't know it now. But I have suggested to my children that they not become lawyers.

When feeling blue about the law, or about myself, I note that even my heroes didn't do all that well. Lincoln was shot and Pete Reiser's career ended when he crashed into the centerfield wall at Ebbets Field. But it was uplifting, almost intoxicating, if even for a moment, to identify with a president of the United States and an All-Star baseball player. It did a little to balance the grimmer truth that I was being supported by the public. Of course, so are the president and the Congress, but they don't look at it that way.

May 10, 1985

A *Minor Character*

Bernard is a minor character in *Death of a Salesman*, but a major bore. That came into focus as I watched the recent revival of Arthur Miller's drama on television. When I saw the original Broadway production thirty-five years ago, Bernard was a wooden figure who clopped by and was soon forgotten. But my years at the bar have sensitized me to portraits of lawyers.

Bernard is a goody-good whose sole function is to be a dramatic foil for Biff Loman, the errant and always disappointing son of Willy Loman (the principal character). Biff is a fine athlete, so Bernard is frail. Biff flunks math, so Bernard is a top scholar. Biff is disobedient to his father, so Bernard is dutiful. However bad poor Biff is in any area, that is precisely where Bernard is oh, so perfect. And as Biff falters into manhood (among other failures, he steals clothes in Kansas City, for which he is jailed), Bernard, to rub it in, becomes a lawyer. And not just any lawyer; when we first learn of Bernard's chosen profession we see him on his way to Washington, tennis racket in one hand, to argue a case before the U.S. Supreme Court. No lower courts for Bernard. I know many lawyers (and other folks) who think that they, too, should start at the top and work their way up from there.

But the point of this essay is to note that despite Bernard's "success" his character may be seriously flawed, even more flawed than Biff's. I base this assessment on one incident: in their senior year in high school, Biff was preparing to leave for the big football game at Ebbets Field; Bernard, then his next-door neighbor, begged to be allowed to carry his shoulder pads, a wish that was granted. If we were to extrapolate on a straight line from then to now, one wonders if Bernard is still deferring to authority, still carrying some very powerful person's uniform.

On the other hand, some pretty important people have been punished for showing independence. For instance Moses, the greatest of Hebrew prophets ("And there arose not a prophet in Israel like unto Moses, whom the Lord knew face to face"—

Deuteronomy 34:10), was denied the right to cross into Canaan because he had once expressed doubt about the Lord's power to bring forth water from a rock (Numbers 20:12). Frankly, I've always thought that Moses' concern was a fair one, because turning on a rock isn't like turning on a faucet, and that his discipline bordered on the unconstitutional. But with that kind of precedent, what heroics should one expect of Bernard, a frail lawyer?

Willy Loman has become a universal symbol for failure, and I once worried that my father might have had similar qualities; he, too, was a salesman who struggled to make ends meet. And he, too, kept up a proud front to strangers. He asked me to change the description of his business on my college applications from "diamond dealer" to "diamond merchant." That was, to me, the functional equivalent of Willy Loman's "smile and shoeshine." But the comparison doesn't worry me any more, because I realize that every man has a touch of Willy Loman, especially to his children.

On further reflection, at least Loman was his own man as he traveled to Providence and Boston to sell his wares. And so was my father, although his territory was more local. I am first beginning to understand that both men knew something that may have escaped Bernard: there was too high a price demanded for success, for crossing into the Promised Land.

October 18, 1985

Purim Then and Now

When I was a child, Purim (which was observed yesterday) was fun. I knew that it wasn't a serious holiday because when it came—the fourteenth day of the Hebrew month of Adar—I still went to school (P.S. 152 in Brooklyn) and my Orthodox father went to work as if it was an ordinary day.

As the Book of Esther was read aloud in the synagogue in the evening, it was the tradition to boo raucously at each mention of the name Haman and to cheer gently at each mention of Mordecai. I ostentatiously took a bow at each mention of my name, which brought catcalls of "Sit down!" from the others, mostly jealous peers with the names of Bertram, Bruce, or Scott. And each year in the temple gymnasium there was a Purim Carnival at which everybody—parents and children—dressed in costume. Again, pushing my one-day advantage to the hilt, I came just as I was, a bona fide Mordecai; and every year the same adults made the same comments, that I was "the real McCoy," a cross-cultural incongruity that I didn't appreciate until years later.

Of course, the story of Purim seemed so simple and so just: Haman had just become the grand vizier of Persia, and when Mordecai would not bow down before him he ordered all the Jews killed. By some miracle, Esther, Mordecai's niece, had just become queen and she asked the king to reverse things; and so Ahasuerus, in the imperial, whimsical way of monarchs (constitutional monarchies had not yet been invented), ordered Haman to be hanged instead. And hanged he was and, poetically, from the very same gallows, fifty cubits high, that he himself had constructed for Mordecai.

The Purim celebration of my Brooklyn childhood ended when the adults (only the men) had schnapps and the children had candy, and everyone danced.

But as an adult, I have come to think of Purim as the grimmest of holidays. Overlooked in the conviviality are some nasty facts: in the rage that killed Haman, his ten sons were also hanged (Book of Esther 9:14); and killed, too, were five hundred soldiers in the palace of Shushan (9:8) and seventy-five thousand "foes" in the provinces (9:16). That is a lot of revenge, considering Haman had actually killed no one. Some cautious civil libertarians might suggest Haman's abrupt end violated the "cruel and unusual punishment" clause of the Eighth Amendment.

If executing Haman and his ten sons, and five hundred guards and seventy-five thousand "foes" in the provinces, was appropriate Old Testament punishment for Haman, who had only plotted evil, what would be appropriate for Adolph Eichmann and John Demjanjuk (the Treblinka guard extradited from the United States to Israel), among perpetrators of the Holocaust?

One can only grope for an answer. The Book of Esther doesn't mention God's name even once, so perhaps the oblique lesson is that the ultimate evil—the plotting to kill a whole people—is Man's work and only Man can resolve it, if at all. Many have commented that the Divine Presence was absent from Europe during the Hitler years.

In thinking about it more and more, perhaps Purim should be celebrated with partying and frenzy, for it celebrates at least that the celebrants are still here.

Pass the schnapps; let it always be Purim.

March 26, 1986

A *Two-Week Vacation*

We told our daughter that she could not take her T-shirt that proclaimed "You Can't Hug a Child with Nuclear Arms"; nor could she pack the less political one that stated, next to a picture of carrots, "This body is all natural. It contains no artificial preservatives, additives, coloring or flavors."

These peremptory editorial decisions were made in response to our tour agency's warning that bureaucratic Soviet customs officials tend to confiscate anything that might be construed as political or religious; and since those officials spoke no English, everything, except an obvious tourist guide to Russia, was usually intercepted.

As our tour of Russia progressed, our haberdashery decision seemed wiser than we knew. Everyone dressed demurely, and there were no controversial messages (shirts, handbills, or posters) anywhere. I tried to imagine how beautiful Red Square in Moscow would be if it were littered with throwaways that read "Save the Whales," or "Out of Afghanistan Now," or "Two Four Six Eight, Mike Gorbachev is a Rusty Gate." But the pamphlets and the T-shirts were as silent as Andrei Gromyko's laugh.

While I had enforced the ban against my daughter strictly, I was determined to be more defiant myself. And so I tried to buy a pocket-sized Bible in one of the Canal Street stores that specialized in Hebrew religious books, a Bible that I could sneak into the Soviet Union. It surprised me that no such Old Testaments were available because I have seen many subway riders reading compact editions of the Scriptures. Indeed, my inquiries brought disbelief: "You want to put the whole Bible into your shirt pocket? Impossible," pointing to some editions that, with their commentaries and footnotes, could not fit into a bookcase. But one store solved the problem: it stocked an edition of the Book of Psalms that was about half the size of a cigarette pack; that was the text that I decided to smuggle across the border to break the Party's atheistic grip.

The problem was one of tactics: should I carry it on my person or hide it in the luggage? I decided to put it in the toilet articles bag, among the many bottles of nose drops that I had brought for the journey. The three of us (my wife, my daughter, and I) tend to sniffle in the summer, and I didn't know if drops or sprays (adult strength) were available to Westerners in the U.S.S.R. The thought was that since the book and the nose drops boxes were of the same size and shape, the camouflage would increase the chance of escaping detection.

We had been warned that passport and customs control took two hours at Moscow's Sheremetyevo Airport and that the search was thorough. During the entire flight from New York I considered what my response would be if the book were found. Should I be truculent and tell them in no uncertain terms that I was an American citizen and could carry a book of the Bible with me any place I wanted to; or should I act surprised and say that I had been looking for that very volume and was grateful that it was finally found (a weak position, I thought, because one doesn't usually place a book among nose drops); or should I just surrender the book quietly and not hold up the line any further? In short, was I going to be like some White Guard counterrevolutionary spoiling for a fight or like an idle Menshevik making an idle point?

As I wondered about my airport response should the book be discovered, I also wondered about the propriety of sneaking a book into the Soviet Union. No one was making me visit the country, and since my visit was both voluntary and a vacation, was I not honor-bound to obey all their laws, whether I liked them or not? I didn't want to be put in the same category as terrorists who claim that their political opinions justified breaking the law. At least the Basques and Tamils usually operated from their own homes against regimes that were imposed against them; but here was I, traveling about five thousand miles to break a law that affected me not at all.

But even in Communist Russia the ancient rule still prevailed—what one fears the most rarely happens. We were whisked through the airport and into the waiting buses before you could say Boris Godunov. But that proved to be the beginning, not the end, of my personal dilemma. For the point I was going to make in defiance of the mighty Soviet Union—the Soviet Union that contains one-sixth of the world's land mass and traverses eleven time zones—was not that I was going to secrete a Bible from the authorities, but that I was going to read it in Moscow, in Leningrad, in Yaroslavl, in Zagorsk, and everywhere we went. I didn't contemplate any public recitation, but just a quiet, personal reading, a quiet, personal contact between me and the officially prohibited past. But I read my Book of Psalms hardly at all while in the U.S.S.R., and guiltily rushed to read more after we landed in Helsinki, our trip's last stop. But by then, of course, it didn't matter; Finland is as free as it is beautiful.

You can buy almost anything in Helsinki's Market Square— vegetables, toys, fruits, furs, fish, clothes, kitchen utensils, flowers, and frozen reindeer meat. The biggest seller was T-shirts, in all sizes and colors, with the forbidding letters "KGB." You don't need a map to know which side of the Iron Curtain you're on. Just go to the town square, and as the young people wander by, read their T-shirts. If the chesty legends are funny, irreverent, vulgar, provocative, preposterous, boisterous, lewd, or just bland political opinion, clap your hands and dance because you're free. Or, if you are so inclined, take out your Bible and "Sing praises to the Lord" (Psalms 9:11).

October 8, 1987

II. *Supreme Court Decisions*

The Quality of Mercy

Any opinion that relies on the testimony of a ghost is bound to be without substance; *Rummel v. Estelle*, decided by the Supreme Court, 5–4, in March, is no exception. Writing for the majority, Justice Rehnquist upheld the constitutionality of a life sentence imposed on a man who was paid $120.75 to fix an air-conditioner that he never fixed. If the same test were applied to television repairmen and automobile mechanics, perhaps the case would have a redeeming aspect; but consumerism was not the Court's purpose.

Anticipating that many people would think that the sentence violated the Eighth Amendment's prohibition against cruel and unusual punishment, the Court underscored that it did not matter that the crime was not violent: "Caesar's death at the hands of Brutus . . . was undoubtedly violent, the death of Hamlet's father at the hands of his brother, Claudius, by poison was not." Yet, observed the Court, all states punish murder by poisoning (nonviolent) as they would murder by stabbing (violent), thereby proving to five men who have never ridden the Lexington Avenue Express at night that the absence of violence is of no significance.

Before analyzing that haunted opinion, we note that the only testimony in the record that Claudius killed Hamlet's father is a statement by an apparition, who claimed that Claudius poured hebenon juice in his ear, killing him at once (*Hamlet*, act 1, scene 5). If the witness had been more corporeal, cross-examination would have established that there is no such thing as hebenon juice, not even in health-food stores; and that nobody was poisoned through the aural canal until the invention, many centuries later, of the presidential primary. So the flat-out statement by the Court that Claudius killed his brother was, on the state of the record, insupportable; it gave weight and credence to blatant hearsay, testimony by a vanishing, ethereal wisp.

Mr. Rummel's problem was, however, not that he disappeared, but rather that he materialized all too often. He is a recidivist, and that's what has done him in. In 1964 he used a credit card intending to defraud another of $80; in 1969 he forged a check in the amount of $28.36; and in 1978 he capped his morbid career of crime by not replacing some air-conditioner filter, or maybe it was a loose switch. In Texas each such crime was a felony; and in Texas if you are convicted of three felonies it's off to prison for life. It's all a matter of luck, because there are many men who have sinned even more than Mr. Rummel but who have been garlanded by the Chamber of Commerce and asked to speak at graduation. Texas must be inhabited by blushing seraphs if Mr. Rummel's indiscretions would warrant a life in jail.

Three opinions were written in the High Court. Justice Rehnquist wrote for the majority; Justice Stewart joined the majority but added a concurrence; and Justice Powell dissented for himself and Justices Brennan, Marshall, and Stevens. The opinions reveal how callous we are, and how illogical is the law.

Justifying a life sentence for Mr. Rummel's capers takes the work, not of a jurist, but of a well-trained magician-logician. The author must establish the theorem that several large and horrendous crimes equal one tiny, almost unobservable, wrong. The logic which confuses big and small is part of our national heritage. How well I remember the local Alfred North Whiteheads establishing, syllogistically, that the Brooklyn College football team was better than Notre Dame's: Brooklyn College beat Susquehanna by 8 points; Susquehanna beat Cortland State by 24 (Susquehanna never did have a good placekicker); Cortland State beat Connecticut by 12 (everybody had a weak placekicker; the story was that all the good placekickers got scholarships to the Big Ten).

At any rate, that made Brooklyn College 44 points better than Connecticut. By a parallel genealogy charge, Notre Dame would be shown to be only 42 points better than Connecticut. Therefore, Brooklyn College was 2 points better than Notre Dame. Similarly, Justice Rehnquist, although he uses fewer steps, equates an unfixed air-conditioner with murder by poison and high (although nonviolent) crimes "in the area of antitrust, bribery, or clean air or water standards." By using the pollution laws as an example, the Court justified sending Mr. Rummel to jail for life; it simply held that all nonviolent crimes were alike. Of course, few people have ever gone to jail for five minutes for violating antipollution laws, although we seem to be putting as much oil in the seas as water.

Another example of the Court's legal reasoning is its use of Argument by Degrees. The prevailing opinion asserts that it does not matter, at least not to the law, whether the amount involved was $120.75 or $500,000, for where do you draw the line? In the way of Socratic questioning the Court asked, if $120.75 was too little for a life sentence, what about $120.76? or $120.77? or $120.78? And if you concede that a long jail sentence would be appropriate if one filched $500,000, what about $499,999.99? or $499,999.98? If this logic were to persist for several days, the up and down numbers would meet, quite meaninglessly, at $249,939.62. Justice Rehnquist argued that there is simply no "objective" place to draw the line, and that $120.75 is as "neutral" a level as any other. If high officials in Washington really think that there is no difference between $120.75 and $500,000, I suggest that we may have found the cause of inflation.

Of the three opinions in *Rummel*, Justice Stewart's logic is the weakest. He uses the logic of redundancy. When you didn't want to do your homework, Mom would end the discussion by intoning, "School is school." Although Justice Stewart acknowledges that the sentence is very wrong, he says (in effect) that it cannot be undone because "The Law is the Law." This may not be the place for a lengthy discussion of the use of precedent in judicial decisions; it is a principle that holds that the first person who decided an issue was, ipso facto, correct. We all have a hankering for the past. But only the law has so institutionalized its nostalgia that change becomes heretical. The basis of Justice Stewart's concurrence was that the Texas recidivist statute had previously been declared constitutional (albeit in a case involving murder with malice). Therefore, he reasoned, he had no "roving commission" to impose his personal preferences on established law. Mr. Rummel suggests that not deciding a case on the merits (thereby sending a petty wrongdoer to jail for life) is just as bad as not fixing an air-conditioner.

The dissent is a rather learned retelling of the history of the

Eighth Amendment citing the Magna Carta, the English common law in 1400, and Section 9 of the Virginia Declaration of Rights. It is excellent, except that it necessarily assumes that there can be a legitimate argument that a man can be sent to jail for life for doing what the defendant did. The majority opinion should have said only this: "It is unconscionable, hence unconstitutional, to send Mr. Rummel to jail for life because this is the United States of America."

One would like to think that *Rummel* is atypical, and that it wouldn't have happened if Holmes or Brandeis or Warren had been about. But *Weems v. United States* (1910), cited by both sides, casts some doubt on that hope. The Philippine Islands had sentenced a man to prison for fifteen years at hard labor wearing chains attached to the wrist and ankle for having made a false entry in an official record. The Philippine court sustained the conviction and sentence, even though no one was injured and there was no intent to defraud. The Supreme Court reversed on the ground of cruel and unusual punishment. But, in what must be the meanest utterance since the witches discoursed on the recipe for their bubbling cauldron (*Macbeth*, act 4), Justice Edward White dissented: "I do not assume that the mere fact that a chain is to be carried by the prisoner causes the punishment to be repugnant to the Bill of Rights, since while the chain may be irksome it is evidently not intended to prevent the performance of the penalty of hard labor."

And, saddest discovery of all, Justice Oliver Wendell Holmes concurred in that dissent.

The law has lost its way if judges are so discomforted by the heat in this world that a broken air-conditioner warrants life in prison. The Court was quick to cite the murders in *Hamlet* and *Julius Caesar*, as if they were somehow relevant to the peccadillos at bar. But not cited was the one Shakespearean verse that addresses the *Rummel* case precisely: "The quality of mercy is not strained; It droppeth as the gentle rain from heaven" (*The Merchant of Venice*, act 4).

May 8, 1980

Waiting

I was thumbing through the most recently published Supreme Court opinions looking for some of those acerbic comments that Justice Sandra Day O'Connor has been addressing to Justice William Brennan, when a footnote caught my eye. It was a curious footnote, and I began to read the text of *Pullman Standard v. Swint,* a case I had not heard of before.

The most important fact of the case, in the context of the footnote, is that it was decided in April 1982. The other basic facts are these: Plaintiffs were a group of black employees. They alleged that the company's (and union's) seniority system was racially motivated and had frozen them into the lowest job categories in violation of the Civil Rights Act of 1964.

In the course of discussing the subtleties of the seniority system, as it was practiced at the Bessemer, Alabama, facility of Pullman Standard, the Court casually, almost nonchalantly, footnoted these additional facts: "The procedural history of this case is rather complex. The original complaint was filed in 1971. Since that time the case has been tried three times and has twice been reviewed by the Court of Appeals."

In its April 1982 opinion, the Supreme Court held that the court of appeals had erred when it reversed the district court; therefore the case was sent back to the district court for a fourth trial. Presumably there will then be an appeal to the court of appeals, thence perhaps to the Supreme Court, which might or might not, at that time, order a fifth trial, from which appeals might, or might not, be taken.

And what must Louis Swint, the black laborer from Bessemer, Alabama, think about all this jurisprudence? We thought it best for him to speak for himself, so we have added a role—only a small role—to *Waiting for Godot.* The play's main characters, Estragon and Vladimir, also know a thing or two about waiting; they've been waiting for the elusive Godot forever:

Estragon: Let's go.
Vladimir: We can't.
Estragon: Why not?
Vladimir: We're waiting for Godot.

Somewhere toward the end of the second act, when Estragon and Vladimir are quibbling about whether or not to move on, Louis Swint enters the stage. He is rather tall, perhaps six feet one or six feet two, and is heavyset; he is in his late forties or early fifties and is wearing overalls and work shoes. Prominently displayed on his overalls is a button that proclaims, "Join the Union." But it is not clear to Estragon, who is always looking for obscure meanings, whether Swint is suggesting that all workers ought to join the CIO-AFL or (with a touch of sarcasm) that the state of Alabama ought to join the rest of the nation. Estragon and Vladimir, who have been bickering and fussing, move off to the side and sit on the ground quietly as Swint slowly but determinedly moves to center stage and speaks:

"You two think that waiting is so hard, and all you do is complain. But your particular wait has been witnessed around the world, and has been translated into dozens of languages. Bert Lahr even played one of you on TV. And when the Israelites waited in the desert for forty years every event was carefully recorded in the Bible, and that exodus is still commemorated by their descendants every year as a holiday. Waiting isn't quite so bad if it is a celebrated event, because then the whole world waits along with you. But when you wait in a footnote, and no one has even heard of the text—that, gentlemen, is *really* waiting."

The soliloquy was over, the footlights dimmed, and Louis Swint exited, leaving Estragon and Vladimir alone on center stage. They wondered aloud, as they discussed the strange interlude, whether Swint's case would be resolved before Godot appeared (as Estragon suggested) or sometime immediately after (as Vladimir insisted).

Said Estragon, reflecting, "I suppose it all depends."

July 14, 1982

No Hall of Fame Niche for ERA Ruling

Despite women's liberation, ERA still means to baseball fans what it has always meant, earned run average.

"How can you say that Koufax (lifetime ERA 2.76) was better than Christy Mathewson (ERA 2.13)?"

"Because Matty played with a dead ball. If Sandy had pitched with a dead ball he'd have had a negative ERA. *They'd* owe *him* runs."

"Well, if Matty could have pitched under the lights in the evening fog his ERA would be lower than the A train."

And so it has raged, the historic American battle of the ERA, among the partisans of Grover Cleveland Alexander, Dizzy Dean, Tom Seaver, Whitey Ford, and my favorite, Mordecai Three-Finger Centennial Brown (ERA 2.06, third best, ever). Now, suddenly, ERA has a new meaning that appears, superficially, to be unrelated to runs allowed by a pitcher without miscues by the defense. But unlikely as it may seem to a coiffured, well-tailored loan officer at the Woman's Bank, the two ERA's are, philosophically, the very same. Both seek to measure people by their ability only, not by their color, religion, national origin, gender, or the shortcomings of others. Baseball's ERA may be ruthless (although Babe Ruth's ERA as a pitcher was a marvelous 2.28), but it is impervious to any subjective tinkering. It measures performance to two decimal places, or more. In this world of rockets aimed at the galaxies beyond, our most sophisticated computer technology is still not as refined or as accurate as baseball statistics. The new ERA seeks to extend to every person the same rights that pitchers have always enjoyed—the opportunity to make the Hall of Fame or the All-Star Team or just the bullpen in whatever is one's life endeavor.

In eliminating artificial barriers, sports is far ahead of the Supreme Court, although the Court is wordier.

The Supreme Court's opinion in *Personnel Administrator of Massachusetts v. Feeney* will not be voted into Cooperstown. That decision approved an artificial barrier for women (and others) that is as high as the World Trade Center, and as square.

Ms. Helen Feeney was denied the opportunity to work for the Massachusetts Board of Dental Examiners because she had not participated in the defense of the Maginot Line or in the invasion of Guadalcanal. That non sequitur of the century became the law of the land when the Supreme Court upheld the constitutionality of the Massachusetts Veterans Preference Statute; that statute gives an automatic preference, in civil service employment, to veterans. And so Ms. Feeney, who scored among the highest in the civil service examinations, but never went to boot camp, was denied the opportunity to work at the Board of Dental Examiners. The new dentists themselves, of course, need not be veterans; most of them probably never even heard of Guadalcanal, a dental desert without one water-pik.

The preference law was challenged on the ground that it denied women the opportunity to obtain any decent civil service employment in Massachusetts. In defense, no one argued that there was any rational connection between once having been a GI and one's ability to process applications submitted by graduates of dental school.

The Supreme Court simply ignored that issue and reasoned that the Preference Law was legal because it was couched in "gender-neutral language." That means that if one didn't chance to know that all war veterans were male, one could not glean from the language of the law that only males would be able to obtain all the important civil service jobs in Massachusetts. Of course, the High Court *knew* that all veterans were male, because that was the very point of the *Feeney* case. But, reasoned the Court, since the *language* of the law was "neutral," the *facts* were irrelevant. By that level of disputation, the Court would consider the Detroit Tigers (who last won a pennant in 1968) to be baseball's fiercest team, and the Oakland A's to be the most scholarly.

The *Feeney* case provides a searching insight into how we, as a society, perceive the sacrifices of war, for the Veterans Preference Statute discriminates against many groups other than women. War orphans and bereaved parents, if they themselves were not veterans, would be denied employment. So, too, persons who were too sick or too disabled to have served. And those too young or too old. Would it be wrong to suggest that even conscientious objectors ought not be excluded from the Massachusetts civil service? Although the Court's opinion is not crisp or brief, none of these other shabby effects of the Preference Law is even considered. One suspects that if instead of a suit by a woman, the Preference Law had been challenged by a polio victim, the result would have been different.

The *Feeney* decision is notable, too, for its original treatment of cause and effect. In nature, the two are inseparable; when it rains, we get wet. But in *Feeney*, the Court held, perhaps for the first time since Galileo was banished, that cause and effect were unrelated. Thus, although it acknowledged that the Preference Law prevented any woman, no matter how gifted, from ever obtaining a decent job in the Massachusetts civil service, the Court defended the law on the ground that such discrimination was not the law's purpose, only its necessary and inevitable effect.

Back in the sixties, there was a button that proclaimed, "If you're not part of the solution you're part of the problem." How could so many unruly and untutored teenagers have a better insight into etiology than the Supreme Court?

Can it be that the law, with its precedents going back to Solon, is less perceptive about discrimination than sandlot athletes? Or is it that sports are unlifelike, because he (or she) wins who runs the fastest, who leaps the highest; no adjustment is made for color, religion, social status, wealth, or whether one wears campaign ribbons. The hardest thing to explain to a youngster today—harder than the new math or the old morality—is how organized baseball could not have had black players until 1947. Sports never deceives because it is all action and no words. Is there a lesson there, somewhere, for the law?

Sports, with its facts, facts, facts, separates the great (Joe DiMaggio's lifetime average was .325; Ted Williams's .344) from local heroes who dreamed of greatness but were only very good (Dixie Walker hit .306). But that separation of opportunity and achievement is not always appreciated by the more emotional ERAers. Men are faster runners than women, and stronger, which doesn't mean that they are better or smarter; after all, a horse runs the mile in under two minutes. But it does mean that men are better tennis players, even though some of the tournament purses are now the same. As a matter of further fact, the abilities of men and women do differ in several areas. Women are superior in languages, whereas men do better in chess, in composing serious music (name a symphony written by a woman), and in mathematics. The women, in a spirited defense, say it is all cultural and not genetic: how can a woman be expected to have written a symphony if women weren't even allowed to study music until the early 1700s?

But I know that the male math proficiency is an acquired characteristic, because I remember those days in Brooklyn, before there were pocket calculators, computing the ERA of Van Lingle Mungo (3.47) by long division, in a desperate effort to prove him better than the Giants' Carl Hubbell (2.97). But when the hard facts are unpleasant, even sports fans can rationalize like the Supreme Court. If one couldn't acknowledge Hubbell's superiority, there was always refuge in words: "If Mungo could pitch in the Polo Grounds, with the centerfield bleachers 505 feet away . . ."

February 4, 1980

Some Impressions of the Law

This essay about Art and the Law begins, improbably, with the arrest of one Mark Royer at the Miami International Airport; he was caught with sixty-five pounds of marijuana. Although by Miami Airport standards that was but a hint, a dash, a twist, the merest smidgen of the stuff, Royer was, nonetheless, charged with a felony. His defense was that his constitutional rights under the Fourth Amendment had been violated because there had been no reason for the narcotics agents to have detained, questioned, and arrested him in the first place.

The case carried to the Supreme Court of the United States, where, in a rather hard-to-follow opinion by Justice White, that defense was upheld. Justice Rehnquist's dissent pointed out, rather cogently, how unrealistic the Court's decision was, for there were plenty of reasons to suspect and arrest Mr. Royer. He was unusually nervous; he had paid for his airfare to New York with small bills peeled from a large wad; he had used a phony name; he had used a phony reason for using the phony name; and finally, he had consented to the opening of his two bulging suitcases, which didn't contain even one toothbrush.

But rather than be satisfied by demonstrating how wrong the Court's opinion was, Justice Rehnquist began to wax eloquent. He did what he so frequently cautions others not to do; he wandered far afield. Among other things, he discussed art en passant: "[The Court's] conclusions are adumbrated, but not stated; if the [Court's] opinion were to be judged by standards appropriate to Impressionist paintings, it would perhaps receive a high grade, but the same cannot be said if it is to be judged by the standards of a judicial opinion."

From which compound sentence I gather that Justice Rehnquist thinks it is easier to paint a picture that hangs in the Louvre than to write a well-reasoned judicial opinion, that almost anyone could be a Renoir, a Monet, a Cézanne, a Manet, a Gauguin, a Bonnard, a Matisse, but that, on the other hand, it takes *real* talent to be a judge. Just dab a little yellow here, a little mauve there, and as long as the canvas appears incomplete, Justice Rehnquist suggests, you may have a genuine masterpiece, or at least something that will fetch six figures at Sotheby's.

Justice Rehnquist's view is worrisome because the noblest part of our law is also impressionistic, so that that school of art ought not to be so readily disparaged. In particular, such mighty constitutional phrases as "due process of law," "equal protection," "just compensation," are as vague as Monet's sunrise over Le Havre harbor (the picture that in 1872 was titled *Impressions* and gave that school of art its name). But nothing can improve on that painting, vague and undetailed as it is; and nothing can improve on "due process of law." Vagueness is essential in these examples of Art and Law, because in each case that means that we, the people, must do the interpreting; our imagination must tell us what our eyes don't see.

Of course, not too many judges have been imaginative; and because of that very few are remembered. I doubt that even legal historians can name any Supreme Court judge who served between the end of Roger Taney's term (1864) and the appointment of O. W. Holmes, Jr. (1902). For instance, in 1872, the year of Monet's *Impressions,* the chief justice of the United States was Salmon Portland Chase of Ohio, a jurist famous today only for his total obscurity; the chief justice in 1902 was Melville Weston Fuller of Illinois, who is even less remembered. Both wrote opinions with such painstaking detail that even the parties to the lawsuits rarely read them. But Monet, Cézanne, and the other Impressionists are still universally recognized, and still dominate Western art.

But Justice Rehnquist's dissent has had one particularly beneficial result; it has raised the level of judicial bickering to new and lofty heights. Justice White, smarting at being called an Impressionist in public, retorted angrily that Rehnquist was a man whose ideas were pre-Columbian. And in the sanctum sanctorum of the Great Court the charges and countercharges began to fly:

"Your opinions are distorted and misshapen. You're nothing but a Surrealist."

"Your views are as meaningless as a Jackson Pollock canvas."

"Don't call me pro-Castro."

"I didn't do any such thing. I called you a Cubist, not a Cuban."

Finally, above the din, it was clear that things had gotten out of hand, that the debate had turned ugly. A voice, some say a woman's, was heard to allege:

"You people are Modern."

The chief justice, ashen, gaveled the discussion to a close and asked that that last remark not be repeated ever again.

Mr. Royer was, I suggest, fairly and legally arrested. He was carting, for next-day delivery, sixty-five pounds of hashish. For him to go free gives us all a bad impression of the law.

May 4, 1983

Odysseus and Mrs. Phinpathya

The essay is about two wanderers, Odysseus and Mrs. Phinpathya. Odysseus had to overcome only "the lawless outrageous" Cyclops (who devoured six of his companions), Circe (who changed his men into swine), Scylla "full of black death," "bloodthirsty" Charybdis, Sirens who enchanted men to death, and a direct hit of Zeus's lightning; those trivial hurdles slowed him only slightly, and Odysseus made it home to Ithaca in ten years. But Mrs. Phinpathya has encountered *real* impediments, for she has had to overcome both the bureaucrats of the United States Immigration and Naturalization Service and the callous law; after fifteen years she is wandering still.

These are the facts of the case: Mrs. Phinpathya entered the United States from Thailand in 1969; her husband had come a year earlier. Their daughter, Nissa, who was born in the United States, has epilepsy and requires constant, and very high level, medical attention.

Mr. and Mrs. Phinpathya had the legal right to stay in our country only until 1971, but they stayed longer (without permission) because here is where they want to live. That made them subject to a new law, Section 1254(a)(1) of the Immigration and Naturalization Act. That section permits an alien to avoid deportation only if he meets both prongs of the law: (1) There must be "extreme hardship" (to the alien or to his family) *and* (2) the alien must have had seven years of "continued physical presence" in America immediately preceding the application.

Since Mrs. Phinpathya had returned to Thailand for three months in 1974 to care for her sick mother, the magic seven-year string was broken. One might wonder about a law that punishes a daughter for being dutiful but, as the imaginative Immigration Service boys explain it, that is Congress's doing. And so the Service rejected Mrs. Phinpathya's claim and began the ominous deportation proceedings.

The Ninth Circuit Court of Appeals (per Reinhardt, J.) reversed, emphasizing the plight of little Nissa. That court understood, of course, that the three-month gap posed a technical, logical problem of statutory construction; but what are courts for if not to interpret laws in a just and humane way. The Ninth Circuit held, in effect, that since it had always been Mrs. Phinpathya's intent to remain in the United States (her husband and child had stayed when she left to care for her mother), and since the native American child, Nissa, would suffer "extreme hardship" if the family were deported, Mrs. Phinpathya had, therefore, complied with both parts of the law. The Service was unanimously reversed.

But the overworked Supreme Court, sensing some threat to the Republic, agreed to hear an appeal, and unanimously reinstated the deportation proceedings. Justice O'Connor, writing for the Court, held that the "extreme hardship" test was separate from the "continuous presence" test and criticized the Ninth Circuit for merging the two. This was the Supreme Court's oxymoronic conclusion: "We do justice to this scheme only by applying [the law] however severe the consequences."

And now I must explain my bias. My reading of the Phinpathya case (decided by the Supreme Court in January 1984) was vividly colored by my just having reread *While Six Million Died*. I read, again, of how the ship *St. Louis* sailed from Germany in May 1939 with 930 refugees (over 400 of whom were women and children) making a desperate exit from the Holocaust. They were within sight of Miami, they saw the flickering city lights at night, but Coast Guard Cutter 244 was dispatched to make certain that no one landed, that no one swam ashore, that no one violated our immigration laws, that no one escaped from Hitler.

On June 6, 1939, a different sort of D-Day, the ship was forced to return to Europe. The passengers, in disbelief, sent a desperate telegram to President Roosevelt. There was no reply. Those to whom England gave refuge lived; but most of the others, who found asylum in Holland, Belgium, and France, were trapped and killed when the Nazis overran Europe. Mr. Roosevelt, some legal experts in the State Department still explain, had no choice, for he was bound by the sacred provisions of the immigration laws.

My father was a devoted Democrat; my Uncle Moe was a pugnacious Republican and a Roosevelt-hater. I remember the conversation as if it were yesterday. It was during a Passover Seder in the early forties, when most of the family children had gone to war; I was too young. As the traditional story of the exodus from Egypt was being retold, my uncle, who was an unusually strong-spirited man, suddenly burst into tears about the ship *St. Louis* and the failed exodus from Germany. He said to my father: "Bernie, if there had been cattle on that ship the United States government would have rescued them on humanitarian grounds." There was, from my father, no response other than more tears, and then a weak refusal to admit that Roosevelt was worse than the pharaoh.

Odysseus survived the Trojan War unscathed, and made it home to Penelope unscathed, because someone in authority, the gray-eyed Athene, daughter of Zeus and conscience for the gods, cared. As that goddess herself put it: "But the heart of me is torn for the sake of wise Odysseus, unhappy man, who still, far from his friends, is suffering griefs" (*The Odyssey*, book 1, line 48; Lattimore translation).

So when the great storm threatened to drown Odysseus, Athene, good to her word, intervened. She "stirred a hastening North Wind, and broke down the seas before him," clearing a path so that her favorite Greek warrior was saved (book 5, line 385). That story reminds one of the events recounted in the Book of Exodus (14:21), when the Lord divided the sea with a strong wind, and the Israelites, fleeing Egypt, were saved.

Therefore, we see that all laws, even the harsh and supposedly unrelenting laws of nature, can be interpreted, modified, or suspended when the need is great. It takes someone compassionate, some Athene. She guided Odysseus through the shoals to safety; may she do the same for Mrs. Phinpathya.

February 14, 1984

Paradise Lost, 9–0

Milovan Djilas was born in Montenegro, Yugoslavia, in 1911 and joined the Communist party as a student in Belgrade in 1929. He rose swiftly in the party ranks, becoming a member of the Central Committee in 1938, of the Politburo in 1940, and of Tito's cabinet immediately after World War II. He twice led a delegation to Moscow, and became vice president of his country. But then his mind wandered, his thoughts deviated, his ideas became original.

Djilas began to question the party's bureaucratic practices and he respectfully dissented when several Soviet divisions tiptoed into Hungary. While in Sremska Mitrovica Prison he wrote six books, including the only translation into Serbo-Croatian of Milton's epic poem, *Paradise Lost*. There are many, many tasks in this world more quickly done than translating *Paradise Lost*, but Mr. Djilas had plenty of time. Altogether, he was in prison for over nine years.

The above is but a prologue to a discussion of *Immigration and Naturalization Service v. Stevic*, a case decided last month by the U.S. Supreme Court, 9–0. Predrag Stevic, too, was a Yugoslav. While visiting his sister in Chicago he met and married an American citizen. That entitled him to a new visa. Stevic's father-in-law had been active in a militantly anti-Communist émigré group, Ravna Gora. His father-in-law, upon a trip to Yugoslavia, was imprisoned for three years because of his thoughts and affiliations. After his marriage, Mr. Stevic also joined Ravna Gora. And then his wife was killed in an automobile accident, whereupon his visa was automatically canceled. The ever-vigilant U.S. government began deportation proceedings immediately.

Section 243(h) of the Immigration and Nationality Act authorizes the attorney general to withhold deportation of any alien who, in his opinion, "would be subject to persecution on account of . . . political opinion." But the attorney general, apparently forgetting where his Serbo-Croatian version of *Paradise Lost* had been translated, refused to act.

Stevic sued, and the matter wended its way through five courts (the Immigration Court, the Board of Immigration Appeals, the U.S. District Court, the U.S. Court of Appeals, and finally, the Supreme Court). As a result of all that intense judicial activity, Mr. Stevic's deportation now seems likely. The main issue in the courts, and the only issue in the Supreme Court, was this dry, grammatical one: Did the statutory words "subject to persecution" mean that an alien could *not* be deported if he had "a well-founded fear of prosecution" (as Mr. Stevic contended), or did they mean that an alien *had* to be deported unless he could prove "a clear probability of persecution" (as the government contended)? The Supreme Court ruled, unanimously, that the stricter government standard applied. One wonders what was the point of the Supreme Court's lengthy, learned but naive parse, since whatever test is applied, Mr. Stevic, if deported, is sure to end up in some Slavic slammer.

Milovan Djilas did not choose *Paradise Lost* by chance or whim, for the poem's symbolism is endless. It concerns not only man's first disobedience (book 1, line 1) but his redemption and ultimate triumph. Djilas must have smiled at his jailers as he translated these lines:

> The mind is its own place, and in itself
> Can make a Heav'n of Hell, a Hell of Heav'n.
> [book 1, lines 254–55]

And the poem has lessons for us, too. Amid all the chaos, "Sin and Death and yawning Graves" (among many places, see book 10, line 635) of this turbulent world, there has been one place of refuge, one Eden. I hope it is not chauvinistic to say that that place has been America. What grand national purpose is served, what law is enforced, by sending émigré Predrag Stevic back to "the gloomy Deep"? (book 1, line 152).

Before deporting Mr. Stevic, our ambassador in Belgrade should speak to Mr. Djilas if, perchance, that Yugoslav intellectual and patriot is free to talk.

July 10, 1984

A *Prayerful Concurrence*

Among the Ten Commandments is the rather bland one enjoining us to remember the Sabbath and to keep it holy (Exodus 20:8). But the implementation of that rather general direction has, surprisingly, been the subject of much controversy, including, most notably, the Crusades (eleventh to fourteenth centuries), the Thirty Years' War (1618–1648), and the disputes in my family when I was growing up (the 1940s).

I often resisted joining my family at Friday night services at the local synagogue because I preferred to listen, instead, to my favorite radio program, "The Lone Ranger." The program, in those years, had a cult following so that even people in high school were avid fans. Since it was a given in my home that Friday night should be a little different, a little less profane, I was forced to argue that "The Lone Ranger" had some religious content, perhaps even enough to qualify a listener as observant, if not Orthodox.

The point was that in "The Lone Ranger" good always triumphed over evil, and in less than thirty minutes. That was, I noted, considerably less time than the forty days and nights of deluge it took to root out evil in Noah's day; and the Lone Ranger's methods were considerably less soggy. Adding to his saintliness, the masked stranger always left the scene of his derring-do before he could be thanked; he was good for good's sake. That, I suggested, was the essence of religion.

Since my points bordered on the atheistic, I am still amazed that I was allowed to hear the radio instead of a sermon. But my almost-Orthodox parents agreed with me that religious observance (including nonobservance) was a matter of conscience which each person had to decide for himself.

That brings me to the Supreme Court's recent opinion in *Thornton v. Caldor, Inc.* On one level, the case stands for religious liberty because it reaffirms our constitutional separation of church and state. But it is not quite that simple, and that is the point of this essay.

These were the facts: the Connecticut legislature had enacted a statute (section 53-303e[b]) which provided: "No person who states that a particular day of the week is observed as his Sabbath may be required by his employer to work on such day. An employee's refusal to work on his Sabbath shall not constitute grounds for his dismissal."

Donald E. Thornton, a devout Presbyterian, chose not to work on Sunday, his Sabbath. But the Caldor store in Waterbury, where he managed the men's and boys' clothing department, was open every day of the week and required him to work about one Sunday a month. He refused to work on Sundays and he also refused to be transferred to Massachusetts (where Caldor stores are closed on Sundays) and he refused to be demoted. Whereupon Mr. Thornton was discharged, a firing that violated the law quoted above.

The Supreme Court of Connecticut, however, and then the Supreme Court of the United States, ruled the statute to be unconstitutional, and Mr. Thornton's discharge (because he worshiped on Sundays) became final. The two high courts ruled that the Connecticut law violated the First Amendment's separation of church and state because it made a religious observance a legal reason for not working; under the Constitution the government must be strictly neutral on all matters of religion.

The U.S. Supreme Court bolstered its opinion with a horrible example: What if a school teacher, or worse still, many school teachers, observed Friday as their Sabbath? And what about other workers who might be irreligious but wanted not to work on Sundays for purely secular reasons? Since the government cannot prefer religion *qua* religion over any other consideration, one must agree that logically, and as a matter of clear precedent, the Connecticut law was, indeed, unconstitutional.

But let us look at the case as it might be viewed on a football telecast, with a reverse-angle lens. We see Mr. Thornton, and only Mr. Thornton, not wishing to work on Sunday because of a personal, compelling religious reason, for which he is discharged.

It really must matter very little to Caldor, a large retail chain, whether this one privately religious man works on a particular Sunday or not; some assistant could surely take his place (as if he were ill). But he was discharged as a matter of constitutional principle. However, what distinguishes the United States above all nations is its devotion to individual conscience, for individual conscience is what the First Amendment is *really* about. It is, therefore, disquieting, even if constitutionally correct, to realize that Mr. Thornton's conscience has been treated no more kindly in Waterbury, Connecticut, than it would be in Moscow, U.S.S.R.

December 13, 1985

How "Cap" Weinberger Got His Nickname

*I was surprised to learn, when I first read the Supreme Court's
decision in* Goldman v. Weinberger, *that "yarmulke" was a word
in the English language. I was even more surprised to learn that it
had become a part of constitutional history. The facts were these:
an Orthodox Air Force officer, a Captain Goldman, wanted to
wear his yarmulke while on desk duty; but the military mind, ever
alert to every threat to the national security, challenged his right
to do so on the ground that uniforms must be uniform. The issue
reached the Supreme Court, which upheld the military's yarmulke
ban. This essay discusses that decision.*

When Pentagon brass received an inquiry from the
March Air Force Base in Riverside, California, as
to whether a desk-bound officer could use a yarmulke, it referred that delicate question to its
Special Committee, with orders to investigate thoroughly and report back promptly. Having no idea of what the subject of their
inquiry was, but ashamed to ask, the committee's officers began a
frantic inquiry. They were unanimous that the term sounded Japanese, and there followed a learned discussion as to whether a
yarmulke was a motorcycle part or a stereo-communication
device (one of those microscopic chips for which Japan was
famous).

One unusually bright lieutenant suggested that it was probably
part of a stereo unit because "yarmulke" rhymed with "harmon-
ica." Contact was made that very night with an attaché in the U.S.
Embassy in Tokyo, who was instructed to obtain, most discreetly,
a yarmulke sample. But the attaché reported that no one at Mit-
subishi would admit to having heard of such a thing, which confirmed to the military mind that what they were seeking was valuable indeed, perhaps the key to Japan's balance of payments
surplus. But further investigation was frustratingly unsuccessful.
The Japanese trail was growing as cold as the Sapporo ski slopes.

Desperate officers called the CIA. They, too, had never heard of a yarmulke, but referred the matter to their linguistic experts; the report back was that the term appeared to be Russian. Pentagon officers were wary, because the CIA (they said) ties everything to Russia, for that is how they keep their budget intact. But a printout from the CIA language computer did show that the yarmulke was derived from Yalta, although no one yet knew exactly what it was, or whether it had been discussed at the famous Big Three Conference that had been held there in February 1945.

Whereupon, one of the CIA inquiries led, unexpectedly, to the zoology section of the State Department. Several international fauna authorities had concluded that the yarmulke was the affectionate name given to a baby llama. But, unfortunately, that could not be confirmed.

Then, along the way, came a call from Agriculture. Their experts believed that yarmulke was a health food, probably a portmanteau word combining yogurt and almonds. At that very moment, department aides were fanning out in San Francisco hoping to pick up samples of low-fat yarmulke.

Despite the massive investigation the committee was still not able to render a definitive report (or even a vague report) to the Joint Chiefs of Staff; and the deadline was approaching. They decided to do the prudent thing, since the security of the Western World might be involved. They decided, unanimously, to ban the indoor use of the yarmulke.

When Captain Goldman of the U.S. Air Force was notified of the ban, he sued on the ground that it violated the First Amendment's guarantee of religious freedom (*Goldman v. Weinberger*). The case was ultimately decided by the Supreme Court, which upheld the ban, 5–4. In his majority opinion for the Court, Mr. Justice Rehnquist, unaware of the process's finer points, held that civilian courts must give "great deference" to the military's "considered professional judgment."

The military's ban on yarmulkes is petty and will probably be changed administratively. Then the only point of this long story will be to remind people how the Secretary of Defense, Cap Weinberger, really got his nickname.

April 14, 1986

The Law's Pitch Is Wide

Although baseball has fixed rules (three strikes and you're out; even a rich kid can't buy a fourth), the game is, nevertheless, one of men not of laws. If you have a Koufax or DiMaggio your team has a good chance to win the pennant; but if the arm is arthritic, or the Achilles' heel is sore, or the players are aging, another contender (with a Gooden or a Clemens) is likely to make it to the World Series. Sports writers summarize the point by predicting every April that the team that has the horses will win. But I've always felt that there was no need for turf clichés, because in clichés nothing can outrank our national pastime, except perhaps for the law, which is the point of this piece.

Some years ago, in 1973, the Free-Choicers won the final game of the season, the big game, *Roe v. Wade*, to win it all, 7–2. But the losers, the Pro-Lifers, had nothing to be ashamed of; they had put up a spirited battle for a team that was then just a first-year expansion team with only two name players. They had Whizzer White, who had lost a step (some say two) from his All-American days, and Bill Rehnquist, then a rookie, although a much acclaimed one. And although *Roe v. Wade* became history, it became history somewhat the way the World Champion Dodgers of 1955 became history; both are there in the record books, but it is not clear if either affects play now, this year. Roe, by the way, was not Preacher Roe, the immortal Dodger left-hander (22–3 in 1951), but Jane Roe, a legal pseudonym for an unwed pregnant female who wanted an abortion although the laws of Texas forbade it. The Pro-Lifers were embarrassed, for no team, not even an expansion team in its first year, likes to lose to a pregnant pitcher.

But times change. Just last month (in *Thornburgh v. American College of Obstetrics*) the Supreme Court's Free-Choicers, showing the loss over the years of Douglas and Stewart, the once reliable middle of the batting order, had their winning margin reduced to 5–4. And when the new season opens in October, Bill Rehnquist, once the much-acclaimed rookie, will be the player-manager, and Nino Scalia, who was the Most Valuable Player in the Triple A Court of Appeals, will start in place of the retired Burger. There are, by the way, differing opinions of whether Burger will ever be elected to the Hall of Fame in Cooperstown because everybody suddenly seems to be demeaning his contribution. Some say that during his seventeen-year tenure he struck out too often with the winning runs on base. For instance, these critics say, he faced Miranda, a pitcher who was faltering in late innings, but he never managed to get the big hit that would have knocked him out. Commentators are quite surprised that it is Burger who has retired and that it is Miranda who is still active, still giving his famous warning to each and every arrested player and fan.

As Jimmy the Greek and other scholarly pundits begin to chart the forthcoming season, they are making the Free-Choicers and Pro-Lifers co-favorites at 6–5, pick 'em. It is the first time since they joined the Big Leagues that the Pro-Lifers have been so highly rated. Some Grapefruit League analysts, pointing to such promising prospects as Bork from Washington, D.C., and Posner from Chicago (both considered Pro-Life farm teams), argue that the tide has begun to turn, as it does for every expansion team. Remember the 1969 Mets.

But, of course, every minor league star isn't promoted to the majors, and with the current roster limitations, there won't be any other promotions soon unless either Bill Brennan (whose rookie year was 1956) or Thur Marshall (class of 1967) retires. And both of these veterans continue to surprise by their steady play, especially on defense against the heavy right-hand hitters. If Brennan and Marshall keep playing until 1989, and if someone like Cuomo or Hart then becomes the Big Manager, Bork and Posner would stay just where they are and some talented young Free-Choicers would be called up to the Supreme Court Nine instead. And then the score might stay at 5–4, in favor of the Free-Choicers, for many seasons to come.

May Day is celebrated in our land as Law Day, and speeches

are made with great solemnity. The one basic theme recited each year, no matter which side has the horses, is that old cliché, that ours is a government of laws, not of men.

July 16, 1986

*Supreme
Court
Decisions*

Sodom and the Constitution

Perhaps because it is derived, etymologically, from Sodom (where the "sin is very grievous"—Genesis 18:20), sodomy has always had a bad reputation. That eponymous fact has also distorted the law, which is the point of this essay. In *Bowers v. Hardwick* the U.S. Supreme Court upheld (5–4) the constitutionality of a Georgia statute that criminalized (twenty years in jail) sodomy. The narrow focus here is on the concurring opinion of Chief Justice Warren Burger. Among the reasons he gave for upholding Georgia's law was that "proscriptions against sodomy have very 'ancient roots,'" condemnation being "firmly rooted in Judaeo-Christian moral and ethical standards." To hold otherwise (continued the chief justice's sermon) "would be to cast aside millennia of moral teaching."

But religious standards vary from place to place, from family to family. I grew up in a fairly Orthodox home, and was always made aware of a wide variety of biblical injunctions. "Honor Thy Father and Mother" was often invoked when they said I should do homework or go to sleep and I wanted to listen to Red Barber's broadcast of the Dodgers game. Night games from St. Louis were a particular problem. But of all the rules I learned, only one was related to sex; that was the commandment against coveting thy neighbor's wife. I understood its popular translation, banning adultery. But even as a child I was puzzled how merely coveting something could be illegal. For, I wondered, how would anyone ever know? Later I speculated that perhaps that was the very point, because surely God would know, proving His presence. At the very least if you were Orthodox you might feel guilty for such lusting and that, in itself, could be the only deterrent that was needed. The mixture of religion and sex gets very complicated.

In all my years of Bible instruction—and I began Hebrew school at age six—I never heard the term "sodomy" mentioned even once. That surprises me now, since the story of Sodom appears so early (Genesis 18 and 19) and was so often told. As I first learned it, Sodom was an evil city (worse even than New York, the teacher said; more like Chicago), although the precise nature of the evil was never explained. But because it was so debauched, the Lord destroyed it with brimstone and fire (Genesis 19:24). The moral was a simple one: evil bore a heavy price.

I did not learn the specifics of the decadence until I was an adult. But by then the story of Sodom was no longer so simple. It begins with a debate between Abraham and the Lord on the fate of Sodom (Genesis 18). The Lord announced that He'd not destroy that wicked place if he found even fifty righteous men. Abraham, appalled at the death of so many innocents, bargained God down to forty-five, then to forty, then to thirty, then to twenty, and finally to ten. If there were only ten righteous men in Sodom, the Lord agreed to spare it.

That simple story presents two complex problems. First, the respective roles of God and Man (Abraham) appear to be reversed. Man might want to destroy the whole place to root out evil (Dresden and Hiroshima come to mind), but a merciful and just God would always find some way to spare the innocent (the way Isaac was spared). But in Genesis (chapters 18 and 19) it was the Lord who sought the total destruction of the enemy, and it was a wise and gentle Abraham, the world's first bleeding heart liberal, who argued for the rights of the blameless.

But there is an even more fundamental difficulty with the story of Sodom: the negotiations between the Lord and Abraham stopped too early. The hard ethical question is: What if there is but *one* righteous man (other than Lot) in all Sodom? Should not Sodom be spared rather than kill that *one* innocent? The difference between fifty and ten sinless men is just a small matter of degree. But the difference between any number and one is a matter of high principle, because then we are dealing with individualism and each man's own right to be respected. But that is the very question that the story of Sodom never reaches.

Sodom may be, on the popular level, a symbol for the utter destruction of evil. But it is, more subtly, also a symbol of power over individuality. For even Lot's otherwise pure wife was killed when she violated the rather meaningless order not to look back. That but underscores the real theme of Sodom—that no variation can be allowed.

Although sodomy is outlawed as an "abomination" later in the Bible (Leviticus 18:22; 20:13), it is done so only as part of a long list of forbidden mixed conduct ("Thou shalt not sow thy field with mingled seed; neither shall a garment mingled of linen and woollen come upon thee"—Leviticus 19:19). The real fury, the "brimstone and fire," is rooted in the story of Sodom, which, as we have noted, has another message.

What makes the parable of Sodom ethically understandable, even in its heavy-handed context, is that it comes so early in the Bible. As the Scriptures unfold, all harshness is tempered. As it is written: "Thou shalt love thy neighbor as thyself" (Leviticus 19:18). "But the stranger that dwelleth with you shall be unto you as one born among you, and thou shalt love him as thyself; for ye were strangers in the land of Egypt" (Leviticus 19:34).

According to the sages, loving thy fellow man, loving the stranger, is the fundamental principle of the Torah, and all the rest is commentary. It is suggested here that Chief Justice Burger, in his opinion in *Bowers v. Hardwick*, may have invoked a vision of biblical "moral and ethical standards" that does not go beyond early Genesis. Although the chief justice believes in interpreting the Constitution according to original intent, I don't think that he meant to go back quite that far.

October 7, 1986

McCleskey v. Kemp

There is a quaint theory of cosmology that is too thin even to have a name, and until the Supreme Court's opinion in *McCleskey v. Kemp* it had no known adherents. The theory is that we have all been placed on Earth just this instant, complete with all our memories and associations.

I first heard mention of that philosophical argument long ago, during a college lecture (assuming, that is, that the theory is not valid). It was a time before computers, and it seemed unlikely that any deity, no matter how accomplished, could mesh billions of memories so perfectly that not one person would be out of sync.

That lecture comes to mind on occasion, especially if I've done something particularly dumb. It is comforting to think that perhaps I haven't done anything dumb at all, but had only been placed in this world a moment ago, complete with the memory of having done something dumb.

Although the Theory of Instantaneousness would exculpate me, it presents problems for others. It would, for instance, cause havoc with the criminal justice system, for it would be blatantly unconstitutional to imprison a man who was not even in existence when the crime had been committed, all the more so since the crime itself was only in society's collective mind. And religion would need new interpretations, because the theory would erase Man's free will and the record of his moral choices; hence the very concept of good and evil would disappear. And worst of all by far, conscience would disappear, for nobody could ever be responsible for anything.

Despite these somewhat negative implications, the theory, which had been dormant for centuries (unless it is valid) received its first written endorsement ever when the United States Supreme Court decided *McCleskey*.

The key to *McCleskey* is its proclaimed lack of any link to the past; that key is hidden in footnote 20. By way of background: In order to prove that the death sentence, as imposed by Georgia, is racially biased, the defense went beyond the mere statistical evidence that showed that a black who killed a white was seven times more likely to receive capital punishment than if their roles had been reversed. Counsel's point was to demonstrate that the 7–1 ratio was not an aberration, was not out of a vacuum. And so it was shown that when the Georgia Legislature reenacted the death penalty in 1972 (to comply with the Supreme Court's new criteria) it did so in the context of a long and dishonorable history of "legal" racial bias.

It was noted that, in the nineteenth century, Georgia even had a dual system of criminal law: if a black woman was raped, punishment was discretionary and doubtful, but if a black man raped a white woman, the death sentence was mandatory; a black person who committed an assault with intent to murder was subject to capital punishment, but the identical crime by a white against a black (even a "free" black) was officially classified as "minor." Although some statutes had to be altered in deference to the Thirteenth and Fourteenth Amendments, attitudes never varied. Desegregation was fought long after the decision of *Brown v. Board of Education* in 1954, and Martin Luther King's challenges were resisted long after his death in 1968. It was apparent to everyone, including Georgia legislators, exactly how the "new" capital punishment law would be applied. Why should anything after 1972 have changed the way the law had been applied for the two centuries prior?

But if the Supreme Court had agreed with that analysis, it might have been required to find Georgia's capital punishment statute to be unconstitutional, because then it would have been a statute with "a racially discriminatory purpose." Rather than reach such a conclusion, the Court simply dismissed the cumulative evidence of two centuries with the bland wave of a footnote (footnote 20): "But unless historical evidence is reasonably contemporaneous with the challenged decision, it has little probative value."

If we parse that sentence it means that there is no such thing as "historical evidence" because once such history is limited to "contemporaneous" events it is, ipso facto, no longer history. The Court's existentialist footnote means that the only things that count are the things that are here and now. It is as if the law had been put on this Earth this instant, out of the void, in strict compliance with the Theory of Instantaneousness. It would have no responsibility for the past and no conscience.

But even if the Supreme Court is correct that the law and its ancient statutes and old precedents and brown-buckram books (with dust and missing pages) and files and reports and opinions and founding partners' portraits (in ornate frames) were all just put here this moment, it would still not justify *McCleskey* and a racially skewed capital punishment ratio of 7–1. It would mean, rather, that the Court, too, was only a millisecond old and that it had a lot to learn about the Constitution.

June 3, 1987

III. *Supreme Court Justices*

Cowardly Lions

In the *Wizard of Oz*, the Cowardly Lion was played by Bert Lahr. Long, long ago, in the real world, that same cameo role was played, although with less wit, by the *New York Times*. This essay is about that long, long ago performance.

By way of background: A few weeks ago, the *Times* ran an editorial entitled "Lions of the Bar." It berated, and properly so, the failure of the bar associations to challenge the rulings of two federal judges, rulings which barred Ms. Cynthia Boston's own chosen lawyer (Chokwe Lumumba, of the Michigan Bar) from representing her. The judges' reason was that they disapproved of Mr. Lumumba's Black Nationalist views. The point of the *Times* editorial, which was well taken, was that had a Wall Street lawyer been barred from the courthouse because some judge did not approve of his politics, all bar associations would have shrieked and howled. In entitling its piece "Lions of the Bar," the *Times* was being as caustic and sarcastic as Old Stuffy can be. The *Times* is no Groucho Marx.

The editorial was a classic case of the pot and the kettle. When I read that editorial, especially the haughty sarcasm, I instantly recalled a book that I had read in my senior year at Midwood High School (Brooklyn), *Brandeis: A Free Man's Life* (by Princeton professor Alpheus Thomas Mason). The early chapters dealt with Mr. Brandeis's youth, education, and legal practice. There was a section on his attempt to challenge something called the Oil Trust; and I was rather glad that he did not fully succeed for the partisan reason that Mobil Oil sponsored the radio broadcasts of the Dodger games. Mobil's symbol, Pegasus, was the closest to Greek culture that most of us came. Dodger outfielders (Pete Reiser, Dixie Walker, et al.) were always (according to Red Barber) riding that "Flying Red Horse" to reach a long fly ball.

But the one chapter of the Mason book that made a searing impression concerned the ferocious fight over Brandeis's nomination to the Supreme Court. The opposition included A. Lawrence Lowell, the president of Harvard, who protested that the nominee did not possess "the judicial temperament and capacity which should be required in a judge of the Supreme Court." Six former presidents of the American Bar Association, including such legal giants as William Howard Taft, Elihu Root, Joseph H. Choate, and Simeon Baldwin, signed a statement certifying that the nominee was "not a fit person to be a member of the Supreme Court of the United States." Think of this: the American Bar Association opposed the nomination of Louis D. Brandeis but formally supported and endorsed the nomination of G. Harrold Carswell.

But what surprised me most then, and what benumbs me now, was the position taken on the Brandeis nomination by the *Times*. Unlike William Howard Taft, the *Times* did not quite have the courage to oppose President Wilson's choice. Rather, it took a "neutral" position, a "fair" stance. Following are some excerpts from the *Times* editorial of January 29, 1916, at page 8, column 1. The *Brandeis* book contains only a small quote from that editorial; I read the full piece at the New York Public Library:

> The familiar question will be raised at once whether Mr. Brandeis possesses the judicial temperament, but the chief and most serious criticism of the nomination will be based upon another, though related, ground. It has been said that Mr. Brandeis would take his seat upon the bench with a variety of preconceived and firmly held opinions relating only remotely, if at all, to questions of law and to the constitutional powers of Government, but rather to questions of a purely political nature concerning social welfare and the social theories upon which legislation might be based. That criticism will be serious, it will have to be met, because the voice of the advocate moved to utterance in behalf of theories of social justice should be heard in the legislative hall rather than in the chamber of the court. The Supreme Court sits not to expound or advance theories or doctrines, but to judge the constitutionality of the enactments which Congress may decree to those or other ends. It need never be said and cannot rightly be said that the court needs among its members some advocate of "social justice." . . .
>
> A radical upon the bench of the Supreme Court is not easily

imaginable. Insofar as Mr. Brandeis's beliefs may have inclined him toward radicalism we must expect the record of his career to be most attentively scrutinized in the Senate.

I still recall the *Brandeis* book so well (although I was graduated from high school during the chief justiceship of Fred Vinson) because it was such a great comfort to me when I went job hunting after law school. Although I had graduated from Brown (Phi Beta Kappa, junior year) and Yale Law School (top quarter), I had a most difficult time finding a position. I tried every major New York City law firm two or three times, but no luck. Every night, in preparation for the next day's rounds, I would type out my résumé (using the two-fingered hunt-and-peck system). I would give the ribbon copy to the firm where I thought my chances best, and so on down the line to the fourth or fifth carbon copy. But whether crisp or blurred, the résumés yielded nothing. My main consolation, after each day's rejections and disappointments, was my belief that "they" would not have hired Louis D. Brandeis, either.

We can consider the Brandeis matter euphemistically and not ethnically and attribute it all to the nominee's rugged individualism. The *Times'* editorial, doubtless written by a committee and subcommittee, conceded as much: "It cannot be doubted that Mr. Brandeis, should the Senate confirm the nomination, would be a conspicuous member of the Court. Because of his ability, the intense interest in the tasks to which he applies himself and the fearlessness in the expression of his opinion, he would be heard from, he would of a certainty attain to great distinction."

But bar associations, the *Times*, and the legal establishment are not always comfortable with individualism. They would disagree, in unison of course, with Thoreau's maxim: "Moreover, any man more right than his neighbors constitutes a majority of one already."

But we note with pride that one gentle and gifted individual (President Roosevelt called him "Isaiah") contributed more to the law than all of his highfalutin detractors combined.

January 22, 1982

Harmony on the Supreme Court

The bickering, cantankerous members of the Supreme Court agree on only one thing: they work too hard. I've not seen all their judicial calluses, but I know that the Court's unbearable sweatshop conditions will continue—nay, may get worse, if that were possible—until the justices do what downtrodden American workers have done for over one hundred years—organize!

One cigar-chomping, fist-pounding, veteran union negotiator will achieve more for the overworked High Court in one bargaining session than all the dainty bar association resolutions and overblown academic reports put together. Our man will argue for some very minimal, nonnegotiable vacation improvements. Specifically, in addition to the skimpy Thanksgiving, Christmas, and Easter recesses, and in addition to the three-month summer vacation (from July 1 to the first Monday in October, every year, recession or depression notwithstanding), the justices need *some* paid holidays.

Various Teamster locals, in an outburst of sentimentality, have won birthdays off for their members; but that would not be practical here because too many lawyers would angle to have their cases heard when this justice or that was home blowing out candles.

What is needed are some neutral, fixed dates when the entire Court would have a paid holiday. Two suggested dates are March 19 and June 5. June 5 (1762) is, of course, the birthday of Mr. Justice Bushrod Washington (tenure: 1798–1829). On that paid day off the justices could consider that being chosen for the Supreme Court is a tribute not only to one's brilliance but sometimes also to one's family connections. March 19 (1891) is the birthday of the late Chief Justice Earl Warren. That day would be celebrated by lawyers as well as judges; and by people throughout the land who remembered when the law was a gentle friend of the underprivileged.

In addition to their demonstrably uncivilized working conditions, there is another, and even more powerful, argument for an easier work schedule; that argument is precedent.

The first Supreme Court met in New York City in February 1790. Chief Justice John Jay gaveled the Court to order, read the Court's brief rules into the official record, and then adjourned sine die. It met again in August, acknowledged a commission appointing one James Iredell of North Carolina to the Court, and then adjourned sine die for lack of business. The February 1791 term was moved to Philadelphia (along with the rest of the federal government) and, after swearing in a few lawyers, again adjourned sine die.

The Congress began to fret that this supposedly coequal branch was getting the edge, especially on Friday afternoons. So the Congress passed a law (1 U.S. Stat. 243, 1792) requiring the Supreme Court to hear all requests for pensions filed by Revolutionary War veterans. It would have been a tedious task, but the Supreme Court did not panic. Rather, it simply held (in *Hayburn's Case*, 2 Dall. 408, 1792) that that law was unconstitutional; and the Court adjourned again for several months.

The present Court will need the same steadfastness, for it is entirely possible that the president would not accede to a union's just demands. The judges must then be prepared to strike. There is a risk, of course, that the president would react the way he did to the air controllers' (PATCO) strike; that is, he'd fire them all. And what would be the consequence for law and justice if, indeed, the Supreme Court were to close? My guess is that nothing much would change. The decisions of the various courts of appeals would then be final, and I would suppose that those decisions are just as good as the Supreme Court's. My own circuit court (the Second Circuit) has had judges just as brilliant as any who ever served in Washington. There have been, just to name a few, Charles E. Clark, Thomas W. Swan (both deans of Yale Law School), Learned Hand, Augustus Hand, and Murray Gurfein.

But that's all philosophical. In the practical world the judges will be spending weary days on the picket lines. At dusk, when they finally put their placards down ("Litigants Please Pass This

Court By"; "Even Criminals Get Some Time Off for Good Behavior"), the Supreme Court Nonet (four basses, four tenors, and one wavering contralto) will gather round the old conference table and sing:

> From San Diego up to Maine
> In every mine and mill
> Where workers strike and organize
> Says he, "You'll find Joe Hill"
> Says he, "You'll find Joe Hill."

The most far-fetched part of this scenario is that it ends with some Supreme Court harmony.

October 4, 1982

A Personal Choice for the Supreme Court

This piece on Judge Robert Bork as a candidate for the Supreme Court was written in February 1985, a year and a half before his nomination.

We come from Vilna in Lithuania, so as between Judge Robert H. Bork of Washington, D.C., and Reb Pinchos-Mendel Singer of Warsaw, I begin with no particular preference. But since sooner or later the president is going to make another appointment to the Supreme Court, it is time to examine the relative qualities—symbolically, of course—of these two leading candidates. They represent opposite views of how a judge should act.

Judge Bork is, of course, very learned. He is now sitting on the U.S. Court of Appeals for the District of Columbia; before that he was a professor at Yale Law School. Reb Singer has a less glittering curriculum vitae; he presided at a Beth Din at No. 10 Krochmalna Street in the Warsaw of long, long ago.

A Beth Din is a court where the local rabbi hears disputes, whether religious, secular, or imagined, between congregants. In the introduction to his book *In My Father's Court*, Isaac Bashevis Singer (Reb Singer's son) described the Beth Din as "an infinitesimal example of the celestial council of justice, God's judgment." A Talmudist would note that it is celestial *justice*, not celestial *law*, that governs. For the celestial laws, which regulate the orbits of planets and galaxies, are considered to be too fixed, too inflexible, to regulate life on Earth, particularly life in the Warsaw ghetto. And so the rabbis of the Beth Din, always worried about being meticulously fair, bend this rule, and that ever so slightly, until a fine justice between the litigants has been achieved.

Judge Bork has recently expressed an entirely different view of the judge's role: "In a constitutional democracy the moral content of the law must be given by the morality of the framer or the legislator, never by the morality of the judge."

That means that the judge should be neutral, absolutely neutral, absolutely amoral, when deciding a case. Law, like the course of Halley's Comet, is all predetermined.

There is much to be said for this more mechanical justice, because why should one unelected magistrate, who may not have been chosen by the Phi Beta Kappa, impose his personal passions, personal beliefs, and personal values on the rest of us? The only problem is that even judges who belong to this Diffident School of Jurisprudence can see things only through their own eyes; and we know how variable that can be. My own first awareness of how subjective is each person's view involved the old Third Avenue El: real estate developers saw it as an ugly impediment and wanted to tear it down, but drifters saw it as a roof.

If we are to follow Judge Bork's principle, it is therefore necessary to devise a system in which judges will be absolutely value-free. And the law, as always, has provided a precedent. When we want juries to be free of all outside influences we sequester them. Similarly, we can sequester judges. The technique is simple if we but have the will: we would choose, at random, several hundred newborn babies each year and place them in a neutral nursery, exactly halfway between the Atlantic and Pacific, exactly halfway between Mexico and Canada, at an altitude exactly halfway between sea level and the top of Mount McKinley. They will grow up without TV, without newspapers, sans anything that could tilt them this way or that. There would be no novels by Dickens, no art by Daumier, no books about the French Revolution or the American Civil War, and no poems by Walt Whitman or Carl Sandburg. The children, as they grew up, would learn only neutral things: mathematics, physics, chess, and music (but not *The Beggars Opera*). Their motto, stamped on all stationery and embroidered on the school flag, would be a quote from Horace's *Odes*, book 2, no. 10, "Choose thou the mean all-golden."

And after fifty of these learned, neutral, unemotional years some bar association committee would select the brightest of the sequestered bunch and ordain them as judges. Although it sounds so easy, there is this hitch: immediately upon their elevation to the bench these pristine judges would lose their innocence. They'd begin to read newspapers and magazines and books and would never again be able to see the world objectively. With each judge hearing only one case before becoming contaminated by the world, the selection process would be very expensive.

Perhaps instead of trying to find or incubate truly objective judges, we should just select judges whose biases we like (as if we ever did anything else). Personally, I favor Reb Singer. He is not pretentious; he knows his limits; he has vast trial experience; and he understands better than almost anyone else that the law is a mysterious link between Man and Heaven.

February 7, 1985

Mr. Justice Scalia and Myrrh

Mr. Justice Scalia still believes, as he did when he was a senior at Harvard Law School in 1960, that the federal courts should be "forums for the big case" only, not the trivia that seems to clog the calendars today (Address to the American Bar Association, New Orleans, February 15). And since he has the evidence—cases filed in the federal courts have increased from 58,000 in 1960 to more than 250,000 per year now—it is clear that some method must be found for separating the Big Case from the Little. And the standard must be objective and fixed or else the very issue of whether a case is Big (hence worthy of federal justification) or Little (for a local court only) will itself be the source of vast and clogging litigation.

The following are several proposals:

1. Big Cases would be those in which the names of the litigants have fifteen or more letters or digits. For instance, the case entitled *United States of America v. One 1982 Toyota SR 5 Pick-Up Truck, Vin: JT 4RN48D9C00039987* (a case chosen from the most recently published Federal Supplement, volume 642) would clearly qualify for the federal court. But such short-styled cases as, for instance, *Roe v. Wade* or *Marbury v. Madison* would not. If this plan is adopted, and its ease of application has earned it strong support among the bar associations, name changes would not be honored for jurisdictional purposes.

2. As an alternative, the actual physical size of the subject matter under litigation might be determinative. For instance, in maritime cases ships such as the *Titanic* or *Queen Elizabeth* would surely qualify but steamboats such as the *Stoudinger* or the *Bellona* would not. The precise cutoff would be a matter for discussion, but perhaps only ships with a displacement of 20,000 tons or more would be eligible, those smaller would not.

As a point of reference, the *Stoudinger* and the *Bellona* were the two steamships owned by one Thomás Gibbons and plied between Elizabethtown, N.J., and New York City. The problem was that the New York State Legislature had granted others the exclusive right to Hudson River traffic, and those rights were owned by one Aaron Ogden. In the great case of *Gibbons v. Ogden*, decided by Chief Justice Marshall in 1824, the Supreme Court established the principle that under the Constitution only Congress could regulate interstate commerce. Ogden's exclusive license was thus voided. But under the test set forth in this paragraph, *Gibbons v. Ogden* should have been ultimately decided not by a federal court but by the Elizabethtown Municipal Court. And who is to say the result would have been different?

3. A third objective test would be the size of the place from whence the litigation arises. Cases from New York, California, and Texas would be permitted; cases such as *Miranda v. Arizona* would not.

The point is that Mr. Justice Scalia's basic assumption—that there is some way of knowing when a case begins whether it is Big or Little—may be faulty. For instance, *Marbury v. Madison* began as a Tiny Case—a bureaucrat on a coffee break refused to perform a ministerial function. But the creative judicial process magically transmuted that case into the Very Biggest Case ever decided, and since then (1803) the laws passed by Congress and by the several states have been subject to judicial review.

And so it has been for most of the litigations we would now describe as "Big." Linda Brown (of *Brown v. Board of Education*) was just the last in a line of millions and millions of American black children who were forced to attend a segregated school, but in that case (finally) the law performed its creative wonders. Clarence Earl Gideon (of *Gideon v. Wainwright*) was indistinguishable from the millions of other defendants accused of a crime who were too poor to have counsel, but it was in his case that the law (finally) held that the Sixth Amendment to the Constitution required the state to provide a lawyer. And Ernesto A. Miranda (*Miranda v. Arizona*) was a typical suspect who had been interrogated by police without having been told of his rights. There had been millions of such persons over the years until the law, so long dormant, finally asserted itself and *Miranda* became a Big Case.

What these cases illustrate is that the law is mostly weeds and underbrush. Only rarely, and after generations of nurturing, does the law finally produce a flower.

As it is written in *The Song of Solomon* (2:11–13):

> For, lo the winter is past and the rain is over and gone.
> The flowers appear on the earth; the time of the singing birds
>   is come, and the voice of the turtle is heard in our land.
> The fig tree putteth forth her green figs, and the vines with
>   the tender grape give a good smell.

Although he never attended Harvard Law School, King Solomon was the wisest of men. He knew that before there could be flowers and green figs and frankincense and myrrh there first had to be the winter.

February 25, 1987

The Spirit of Gunning Bedford

During the long process of filling the Supreme Court vacancy occasioned by the retirement of Justice Lewis F. Powell, the president and the Senate acted exactly as the revered draftsmen of the Constitution had envisioned; they acted disgracefully.

Having agreed on the powers of the Executive (Article I) and the powers of the Legislature (Article II), the delegates to the Constitutional Convention focused next on the selection of Supreme Court justices.* Several members proposed that that power of appointment be given to the president. But the opposition to that idea, led by Gunning Bedford of Delaware, was fierce.

Mr. Bedford declared that there were "solid reasons against leaving the appointment" of Supreme Court justices to the president because it "was chimerical" to think that, in choosing judges, a president would act responsibly. Oliver Ellsworth of Connecticut agreed, and added that a president was not the proper person to select judges because he was "too open to caresses and intrigue."

And George Mason, who had authored the Virginia Bill of Rights, told the convention that to allow a president to nominate the members of the Supreme Court would be "a dangerous prerogative." Those arguments were persuasive and, in its first poll on the issue, the convention voted six states to two against having the president choose the justices of the High Court.

The problem was that the convention did not think any better of the Senate than it did of the president. When it was suggested that the Senate should choose the members of the Court, Nathaniel Gorham of Massachusetts objected, arguing that that would "give full play to intrigue and cabal" and would result in "a mere piece of jobbing." Edmund Randolph of Virginia agreed, noting

*The facts concerning the Constitutional Convention, and all the quotations, are taken from *Notes of Debates in the Federal Convention of 1787 Reported by James Madison* (Athens: Ohio University Press, 1966).

that legislative appointments "have generally resulted from cabal."

In desperation, and unwilling to trust either branch of government, the convention agreed to a negative compromise: the president would nominate, but subject to Senate approval. But the clearly articulated original intent was to find some objective, non-partisan, uniquely American technique to select as Supreme Court justices the very best people available.

The one uniquely American system that virtually guarantees that only the best candidates will be chosen is spring training. It doesn't matter what the Judiciary Committee says or the FBI or the ACLU or the Right-to-Lifers or the American Bar Association or the National Organization for Women or a group of professors from Yale Law School or the National Rifle Association (although that's not so clear) or even the Association of Yuppies. If the man can play the game he makes the team and heads north for Opening Day; but for any left fielder who can't hit, or shortstop who can't field, it's down to Peoria. Judgment is swift and sure, and the only test is ability.

And so, whenever there is a Supreme Court vacancy, all candidates should assemble in Vero Beach at the sacred Dodger training camp. It will soon be apparent to the whole nation who can move to the left and who to the right and who the heavy hitters really are, and who can't handle the hard ones; it would be completely objective. A candidate's regional, ethnic, or academic background would not count at all; only his (or her) talent.

Why should baseball players be chosen with more care and more honesty than Supreme Court justices? This is not meant to be a reflection on any particular justice but on the process from the beginning. Unlike All-Star ballplayers, whose deeds and statistics are universally recognized and admired, most of the Supreme Court justices in our history are unknown, even to the most bookish legal scholars; they are unknown because they haven't made even the slightest dent on the law. Of the 103 judges who have served so far (the successor to Justice Powell will be number 104), only a relative few have been standouts. My guess is that not even a law school librarian could name ten justices from the past (before, say, 1932). There were John Jay, Marshall, Story, and Taney; and there were Holmes, Hughes, and Brandeis. But who would recall Gabriel Duvall; David Davis; Nathan Clifford; George Shiras, Jr.; Howell Edmunds Jackson; Henry Billings Brown; or Mahlon Pitney? Or scores of the other unknown justices like them, justices who have comprised a majority of the Court at all times?

Unless we transfer the powers of the presidency to the commissioner of baseball, the nation's major leagues will continue to be more carefully selected than our Supreme Court justices. Since such a transfer is unlikely (the commissioner already has enough to do), we will probably have to continue with the constitutional system we have had for two hundred years. But then we must confront the dilemma that was not resolved at the Constitutional Convention—how to select the very best candidates for the Supreme Court when the president (generically speaking; not singling out any one president) and the Senate (generically speaking) have lesser, more personal goals.

Perhaps before any president names a Court nominee, he should be made to look the Spirit of Gunning Bedford square in the eye and say to him, without fingers crossed: "Sir, I sincerely believe this appointment proves you wrong."

November 27, 1987

IV. *Some Modern Trials*

Jean Harris and Orestes

On the evening of March 10, 1980, Jean Harris drove from Virginia to Purchase, New York, slipped into the house of Dr. Herman Tarnower, her sometime lover, and shot him to death; after a trial lasting twenty weeks the jury convicted her of murder.

Once upon a time, in ancient Greece, Orestes, after brooding upon it for years, slipped into his mother's house and slew her; after a trial of several hours, the jury acquitted him.

I think that both verdicts may have been wrong. This is an essay on the two murder trials, as reported in *Mrs. Harris*, by Diana Trilling, and the *Oresteia*, by Aeschylus (the Robert Fagles translation). In the telling, Orestes has all the advantage.

Before I discuss their differences, the two trials do have a few apparent similarities. Both involved murders where the motive was personal revenge. And both were close cases, where no one could predict the jury's verdict. That is the strangest part, because there was never any doubt that Jean Harris and Orestes each committed the foul deed. Why, then, should the outcomes have been in doubt? If Dr. Tarnower or Clytemnestra had been killed in holdups by thugs who didn't know them, there would be no conflict to resolve; the murderers would be dispatched without the fanfare of a book (such as it is) or a play (perhaps the greatest ever written). But only because the murders were caused by revenge and hate were the cases close ones.

What is so wonderful about revenge and hate that the law honors them as excuses for murder? The fault is the *Oresteia*'s, for it was written some 2,500 years ago and is the West's first precedent on the subject. It has resulted, at least philosophically, in a great deal of woe in our century, because the one step after murdering people you personally hate is murdering people you don't know but who represent an idea you hate. And so the Archduke Ferdinand was shot at Sarajevo, and the Great War began; and now there are terrorists adrift in the world who kill people they don't know and are considered heroes by their comrades. It may be unfair to blame the jury that freed Orestes for the IRA, the PLO, the FALN, and the Croatian nationalists, but precedents in the law often lead to strange results.

But our purpose is not politics but to explore why Orestes was acquitted and Mrs. Harris found guilty. It's too easy to say that it was because Orestes had no lawyer; and it's too flip to say that Orestes did not have to contend with daily tabloids and the 11 o'clock news. There are, rather, two other reasons I'd like to discuss, a surface reason and a deeper (but very troublesome) one.

The apparent reason for Orestes' acquittal is that he was so straightforward. He not only stated, he proclaimed, that he killed his mother because she had killed his father, Agamemnon: "I drew my sword-more, I cut her throat . . . and to this hour I have no regrets" (*Eumenides*, lines 598 and 602).

Although he had no lawyer, Orestes did hedge his bet ever so slightly: for, in addition to taking the blame himself, he also implicated the gods Zeus and Apollo for commanding him to act.

The jury had to decide a moral issue (such as it was), but not a factual one. The trial at Aeropagus was over in a few hours.

Not so at White Plains. The jury there was given thousands of niggling facts: How thick was the glass in the window? How was the bathtub chipped? Can fitted sheets become dishevelled? From what part of Dr. Tarnower's body did this or that fragment of skin come from? Was the doctor's buzzer working? Where were his eyeglasses? When did Mrs. Harris wash her blouse? How often did Mrs. Harris stay over at the Tarnower house in 1967? What changes had Mrs. Harris wrought in the house's furnishings (she had bought a bird print for the guest room, curtains for the living room, towels for the bathroom, and a dessert dish; and she had reupholstered one chair).

On some of these crucial questions, both sides had experts: the glass would deflect the bullet this way or that; the skin sample was from the hand or the chest and was near or not near the wound. (Had Pallas Athena, the presiding judge at Orestes' trial, drawn the Harris case assignment, she would have ruled out a lot of evidence as irrelevant.) Perhaps—one never knows, of course—Mrs. Harris would have had a happier fate if her trial had not been quite so trivialized. All of Dr. Tarnower's duplicity was somehow lost amid the neat piles of exhibits.

But a more troublesome reason for Orestes' good fortune and Jean Harris's bad may be their relative places in this world. Orestes, son of Agamemnon, was a prince of enormous wealth and power. Upon his acquittal, he said of himself: "He lives again, the man of Argos lives, on his father's great estates" (*Eumenides*, lines 770–772).

Mrs. Harris was of humbler means; she was not a member of any Establishment. It was the dead doctor who had belonged to the country club and who had lived in a mansion with a small lake.

Is it really true—or only an unfair, cynical observation—that when a poor person commits a crime, all juries are devout believers in free will. And when the strong do wrong, the blame is often shifted to some mysterious Zeus.

December 18, 1981

Abscam and Tyrescam Compared

Arecent English case, *R v. Braithwaite* (reported at 2 All England Law Reports 87 [1983]), puts Abscam in a new perspective. The facts of that reeking British scandal are these: The defendant, one Frank Wilson Braithwaite, was a minor functionary at British Steel Corporation. Because British Steel had been nationalized, the defendant was, through no choice of his own, a government employee; and that was the poor chap's undoing. According to the indictment, he had received "some nine motor car tyres" that were paid for by someone else, a someone doing business with British Steel. For that indiscretion he was criminally charged with having violated the Prevention of Corruption Acts of 1906 and 1916.

Despite a vigorous and imaginative defense—it was argued that the Crown's case was inflated; that it was circular; that the prosecutor misspoke; and that he was treading on thin legal ground—Mr. F. W. Braithwaite was, like all the Abscamers in America, found guilty.

Although there are many similarities, this essay will focus on some of the differences between Abscam and Tyrescam. For instance, it took a promise of $10 million to seduce Senator Harrison Williams; Congressmen Myers, Lederer, Murphy, and Thompson refused to budge for anything less than $50,000 each; Congressman Kelly scorned any sum smaller than $25,000; and even a Philadelphia city councilman, who had very few favors to bestow, had the dignity to insist on $10,000. But it took only a few Michelins to corrupt that venal Englishman. It is thus obvious that American public servants have considerably higher standards than do the British.

Before we become too smug, we should note that scandals in America and scandals in Britain must be judged according to those countries' respective judicial scales. It is only some four hundred miles from John O'Groat's on the northern tip of Scotland to Dover on the English Channel; there are small ranches in Montana and Texas that are bigger. If English justice were calibrated to those Lilliputian dimensions, nine tyres (especially if they were whitewalls; the record doesn't say) may be more of a bribe than we think. On the other hand, the millions of illegal dollars spent on Abscam may not be so outrageous when measured against the snowcapped Mount McKinley (20,220 feet).

Ours is a large and lusty land, and Abscam is part of that tradition. It is too bad for the Old Country, but Teapot Dome or Watergate could never happen there, for there is simply no room on that small and crowded island for scandals of such magnificence.

But the most important difference between Abscam and Tyrescam is that Abscam seduced the innocent. Mr. Braithwaite, on the other hand, did what little wrong he did entirely on his own; no Scotland Yard spooks stayed awake nights concocting bizarre schemes to tempt and entrap him. No one said, "If Braithwaite doesn't accept nine tyres, try ten."

The moral dilemma of seduction, posed by Abscam, is most wisely considered in the Good Book, in the parable of Adam and Eve (Genesis 3:1–9). Those who yielded to temptation, Adam and Eve, were, like the Abscamers of our time, punished eternally.

But Genesis teaches a more profound lesson, that those who seduce the innocent must suffer, too. Thus, the serpent was punished the most severely of all: "Because thou hast done this, thou art cursed." (Genesis 3:14). If that impeccable moral logic were applied to Abscam, what punishment should be meted out to those who dangled not an apple but millions of illegal dollars in front of previously innocent people? This is not to suggest that those who tempted and duped our elected officials ought necessarily crawl and eat dust forever. But if convicted Abscamers were to call them snakes they would only be quoting from the Bible.

August 5, 1983

Birnam Wood and General Groves

The Rosenbergs, like the Macbeths, had traitorous designs; and like the Macbeths, they paid the price. This essay will focus, however, not on the many similarities, but on several basic differences between the dark events that were played out in New York in the 1940s and 1950s (as described in a new book, *The Rosenberg File*, by Ronald Radosh and Joyce Milton) and the dark events in Scotland many centuries ago (as described by William Shakespeare).

The Rosenberg File, although lavishly praised, has one serious flaw. It records all the thousands and thousands of relevant facts, including many learned from recently opened government records, in a monotone; all facts are treated equally. But almost buried on page 449 (the *File* has 470 pages of text and 138 pages of notes) is one fact that to me is as dramatic and astounding as the report that Great Birnam Wood was moving to Dunsinane (*Macbeth*, act 5, scene 5): The *File*, at page 449, quotes General Leslie Groves (who was the director of the Manhattan Project that built the first A-bomb at Los Alamos) as follows: "I think that the data that went out in the case of the Rosenbergs was of minor value."

"Of minor value"! That is a rather muted assessment of the Rosenbergs' "crime of the century." The trial judge, when he sentenced them to death, described their crime as "worse than murder" and told them that they had "caused . . . the Communist aggression in Korea, with the resultant casualties exceeding 50,000 and who knows but what that millions more innocent may pay the price of your treason."

But stranger than even the witches' brew of lizard's leg and howlet's wing (*Macbeth*, act 4, scene 1) is the fact that the blame for the discrepancy between the general's assessment and the judge's was the Rosenbergs themselves. When the government introduced the supposed fatal diagram at the trial, the diagram that the defendants had passed on to the Russians (Trial Exhibit 8), the *defense* rose and demanded that it be impounded and sealed so that its fatal secret would never escape. Therefore the court, and all the rest of us, naturally assumed that Exhibit 8 was the real thing. But the *File* now describes it as "comparatively babyish" for, after all, it was drawn by an army mechanic (Greenglass) who had never gone beyond high school and who knew nothing of even rudimentary physics. Ironically, only the Russians, the recipients of Exhibit 8, knew its worthlessness. For Klaus Fuchs, a world-renowned physicist who had worked in the highest echelons of Los Alamos, had already betrayed us. Ironically, too, the British gave their master spy, who indeed may have changed the course of history, a prison sentence of only fourteen years.

Before Macbeth murdered Duncan he mused fretfully on the deed:

> Is this a dagger which I see before me,
> The handle toward my hand? Come, let me clutch thee.
> I have thee not, and yet I see thee still.
> Art thou not, fatal vision, sensible
> To feeling as to sight, or art thou but
> A dagger of the mind, a false creation,
> Proceeding from the heat-oppressed brain?
>
> [act 2, scene 1]

General Groves's belated testimony would seem to have reduced the Rosenberg crime to a failed attempt of their perverse hope and dream of stealing the secret of the bomb. It was, as it were, but a "dagger of the mind," which is quite different from Macbeth's crime, which put the dagger in a back. If you don't think there is a difference, see Duncan.

The Rosenbergs bore their execution so well because they really thought that they had achieved the impossible; little people, through furtive diligence, had (they thought) found and passed along the world's most important secret. But, in fact, it was part Walter Mitty and part Zelig, and hardly a smidgen of Klaus Fuchs. The Rosenbergs, or course, received daily confirmation of their awesome deed from the press, which assumed (as did we all) that Exhibit 8 was real. There had been some previous testimony that had questioned the value of the Rosenbergs' data, but that evidence divided on political, not scientific, grounds. General

Groves's statement is the first of its kind given by someone on the government's side, hence its profound significance.

The Rosenberg charade led to very intricate legal questions: Was the death penalty proper? Was the evidence against Ethel Rosenberg strong enough to convict? Did the Atomic Energy Act of 1946 (which required a jury recommendation for the death sentence) or the Espionage Act of 1917 apply? (Note that Supreme Court Justices Douglas, Frankfurter, and Black, in futile dissents, all thought the Atomic Energy Act applied and that, therefore, the death sentence was illegal.) Could the defendants have been given a fair jury trial considering the atmosphere at the time (Senator McCarthy was on the scene, the press was at work, and the jury was not sequestered)? Did the United States Attorney prejudice the defendants unfairly when he arrested another alleged atomic spy, with great fanfare, during the trial? All of these questions have been bitterly debated for thirty years, always on the assumption that the Rosenbergs had passed the atomic secret to the Russians. If General Groves is correct, the great unending debates have been "full of sound and fury signifying nothing" (*Macbeth*, act 5, scene 5).

Macbeth has been produced tens of thousands of times. In each instance, at the end of act 5, scene 8, Malcolm, the rightful heir to the Scottish throne, invites all to attend his coronation at Scone. Whereupon all the players exit as the final curtain falls. Perhaps the biggest difference between Macbeth and the Rosenberg case is that even after thirty years, the case still lingers. The curtain never falls because each new book suggests more questions than answers. For instance: Where was General Groves during the trial?

October 20, 1983

Gulliver's Visit to Foley Square

This is the only essay that I've written to help a friend win a case. I knew, of course, that it was wildly egotistical to think that the United States Supreme Court would take note of a piece that I wrote for the New York Law Journal, *but the idea of it was fun. My friend Ed Labaton had helped to write the "friend of the Court" brief submitted by a group of religious and community organizations challenging the right of a local school board to ban books from a high school library; among the exorcised writings was Jonathan Swift's classic "A Modest Proposal," the subject of this piece.*

The trial court upheld the school board's right to ban; the appellate court reversed 2–1; and this article appeared the week that the case was heard by the Supreme Court.

My name is Lemuel Gulliver and I have, dear reader, previously reported in some detail upon my various travels. I have visited Lilliput, where the people were so small that six of them danced on the palm of my hand; and I once put ashore on Brobdingnag, where the people were so large I was carried about in a servant's lapel pocket. I am constrained to add this new chapter because when I debarked at my latest port of call—Foley Square in America— I experienced the most remarkable and unbelievable adventure of all.

In fairness, I must give a word of background, lest I be accused of bias or worse. The focus of this essay, Mr. Jonathan Swift of Dublin, is my creator. I would like to believe that I would write with similar indignation were Mr. Swift a total stranger but I am, in fact, much in his debt.

But now to describe my most recent adventure, in the land across the Atlantic. America has many high buildings, not unlike Brobdingnag. One of them, with a great, pointed, golden dome, is the federal courthouse in Foley Square. I journeyed there as soon as I arrived in New York because I was eager to determine whether the bizarre story I had heard by word of mouth from sailors returning from the New World was true: that in America they were actually banning one of the literary works of my own creator, Mr. Jonathan Swift of Dublin.

There follows now, dear reader, an account of a law case actually being litigated there—the case of *Pico v. Board of Education, Island Trees Union Free School District.* The principal facts, ignoring for the nonce the all too many minutiae with which all litigation is sprinkled, are these: one dark night, a committee of intellectual Yahoos invaded the local high school and found on the library shelves eleven books that another committee of Yahoos had once found to be objectionable.

I am not going to pass individual judgment on ten of those books, because they were written long after my time, and Mr. Swift's. I have heard from others, whose opinions I highly value, that these other books are all quite estimable; favorable comments, particularly, have been rendered on *Black Boy* (by Richard Wright), *Slaughter House Five* (by Kurt Vonnegut), *Soul on Ice* (by Eldridge Cleaver), and a book of short stories edited by Mr. Langston Hughes, one of the most distinguished poets of the twentieth century. But, of course, none of these has yet achieved the eminent status of "a classic," for that phrase is reserved, and quite properly so, only for works that are still acclaimed after a century or two. Such a work is the marvelous satire written in 1729 by my own creator, Mr. Jonathan Swift of Dublin.

Appalled by the desperate conditions of the good people of Ireland—and I must note, parenthetically, that things have not changed much lo these last 250 years—Mr. Swift wrote a brief, but entirely devastating, essay, "A Modest Proposal for Preventing the Children of Poor People in Ireland from Being a Burden to Their Parents or Country." Mr. Swift, then the dean of St. Patrick's Cathedral (in Dublin), suggested the following plan to solve the perennial burden of so many lovely, but poor, Irish children: that 100,000 of such children be selected and sold as food, a delicacy. As Mr. Swift put it:

> A Child will make two Dishes at an Entertainment for Friends; and when the Family dines alone, the fore or hind

Quarter will make a reasonable Dish; and seasoned with a little Pepper or Salt, will be very good Boiled on the fourth Day, especially in Winter. . . .

I grant this Food will be somewhat dear, and therefore very proper for Landlords; who, as they have already devoured most of the Parents, seem to have the best Title to the Children.

The essay had such an impact on the absentee politicians and absentee landlords of the day that they actually almost did something to improve the lot of the good, and most deserving, Irish people. And for the next 250 years that noble and witty and biting essay has been like the conscience of Ireland, reminding indifferent officials that their indifference has been noted in the permanent and honored literature of the Western world.

At least it had been part of our literature until 1976, when, in a rather awkward bicentennial observance of America's Independence, the school board of Island Trees Union Free School District No. 26 formally withdrew Mr. Swift's satire from the local high school library. Fortunately, some brave citizens who reside there (led by a Mr. Pico) sued in federal court to have that noble work (and the other works, aforementioned) restored to the library shelves.

The case of *Pico v. Board of Education, Island Trees Union Free School District* was originally heard in a federal court designated as the Eastern District of New York. The judge's decision is one I have been pondering since it was first rendered. I shall try to explain it in but a few words, although the hearing consumed hundreds of pages of technical legal arguments. The plaintiff, a Mr. Pico, was a high school student; he alleged that the school board had violated his rights under the First Amendment to the American Constitution. You may recall that when the Colonies broke away they insisted on writing all their rights down; and the most important of those rights, the freedom of speech and expression, was carefully incorporated into their First Amendment. When I learned that a group of citizens instituted a suit I cheered, for I was confident that Mr. Swift's essay would very soon be restored. But rather than agreeing with those who protested the banning of

Mr. Swift's immortal essay, the district court agreed, instead, with the school board. The court reasoned that since the removal was not based on any religious bias or economic theory it was, therefore, permissible. The court's logic is contained in these two sentences: "Here, the Island Trees School Board removed certain books because it viewed them as vulgar and in bad taste, a removal that clearly was content-based. Whether they were correct in their evaluation of the books is not the issue."

I have reread those sentences dozens of times, but they are still unfathomable. They seem to say that the school board can remove any books it deems to be "vulgar and in bad taste" (sentence 1 in quotation above), although whether or not they are in fact vulgar or in bad taste "is not the issue" (sentence 2 in quotation above).

When I learned that the decision was to be appealed, I made a hasty plan to go to New York in America forthwith. The appellate argument was heard in the Court of Appeals for the Second Circuit, located in Foley Square, in New York. Three judges heard the case, and each of them wrote a separate opinion. Unlike Mr. Swift's banned essay, I venture to say that none of the opinions will become a classic. All that needed to be said could have been said in a few words: "The banning of Jonathan Swift's historic essay was outrageous and is hereby overruled."

Two judges voted, more or less, to reverse the ban. But the strangest of arguments was made by the dissenting magistrate, who voted to affirm the ban. He reasoned that the ban was not so deleterious because the students and teachers could still continue "to discuss in or out of school the ideas contained in the discontinued books"; the only thing the students could not do, he pointed out, was to read the withdrawn books. One may wonder how faculty and students can be free to discuss the ideas of a book which the students have been, by fiat, prevented from reading. To solve that dilemma I, too, have a Modest Proposal: The faculty would assign the students to read all the rest of the books in the world. Since none of them contains any of the ideas that are included in Mr. Swift's brilliant essay "A Modest Proposal," the students will necessarily know, by the sheer force of logic, that any ideas that center around solving the Irish problem by using children as entrées must have come from Mr. Swift's pen. Thus, without ever having to read that ten-page essay, the students would know from whence the essay's ideas originated.

Although the appellate court did, formally, reverse the ban, even that modest reversal has itself been appealed to the United States Supreme Court, which heard arguments this week.

I kept wondering—and I wonder still—what will happen to *Gulliver's Travels* if "A Modest Proposal" is banned. I recall several incidents described in *Travels* that might appear to a person not appreciative of the nature of satire to be, in the court's language, "vulgar and in bad taste." I remember, for instance, how in Lilliput I myself put out a fire by using my own natural water; and I recall descriptions of some indelicate nudity in Brobdingnag. But I ought not focus on them unnecessarily, for fear of attracting them to the very vigilant attention of school boards in America. Could it be, I thought, that they would actually remove *Gulliver's Travels* from hundreds or thousands of libraries in the New World? And in thinking of that I became smug. For what, I wondered, had been the purpose of so violent a Revolution against good King George III in 1776 if the Colonists' liberty had come to this.

March 5, 1982

Claus von Bulow and Shelly Levene

Aristocratic, Danish-born Claus von Bulow (accused by the state of Rhode Island of having twice tried to murder his wife; she is now in a coma from which she is not likely to emerge) speaks five languages, none of which is Chicago guttural. Shelly Levene (the main character in David Mamet's new Pulitzer Prize play, *Glengarry Glen Ross*) is a real-estate salesman who speaks Chicago guttural only. Each man is in trouble with the law. The point of this essay is to suggest that their respective elegance must seem to a layman to make all the difference.

Both are portrayed as greedy, in ways and amounts appropriate to their station. Von Bulow (according to the authorities) first carefully explained to doctors the misinformation that his wife suffered from hypoglycemia, and then injected her with insulin, confident that it would not be detected. Levene was accused of stealing and then selling some "leads" (for prospective real-estate buyers) from his firm's locked files, and then of having crudely broken some windows to make it appear like an outside job. Von Bulow, who looks and acts like Charles de Gaulle, would have inherited $15 millon had his wife died; Levene, who has the chubbiness and character of a ward-heeler, risked all for $2,500, cash.

The Supreme Court of Rhode Island, after reviewing the evidence, confirmed the jury's finding of guilt: von Bulow "decided to take matters into his own hands, one of which held a syringe containing a copious quantity of insulin, and so injected the contents of the syringe into his wife with the intent that she should expire." Nonetheless, in the strange, unfathomable ways of the law, the court reversed his conviction. It held (among other legal points) that von Bulow's constitutional rights under the Fourth Amendment had been violated.

At the center of this impermissible search and seizure was "the black bag," the bag that contained not only the fateful insulin-tipped needle but other more ordinary drugs (tranquilizers and anesthetics).

Martha von Bulow's son, Alexander, a college student, became suspicious upon his mother's second coma and returned to Clarendon House, the family's lavish Newport estate, with a private detective and a locksmith from Providence. They searched von Bulow's closet, desk, and study in the middle of the night; when they found the black bag, they took it with them back to New York. The syringe and needle were sent to a lab, which disposed of them after the analysis; the analysis was that the needle had been used for insulin injections. The Rhode Island police were then notified, and the black bag and the rest of its contents were delivered to them. Thus began the investigation that led to the trial, conviction, and reversal.

The police stored the black bag under lock and key, and within a few weeks sent some of the contents out for further chemical tests. From those innocent, routine, extraordinarily ordinary facts, the court found that the defendant's constitutional rights had been trampled on.

I will leave for the law reviews a fuller analysis of the Fourth Amendment claim. We note, however, that the judges were unanimous that the amendment did *not* apply when Alexander searched von Bulow's rooms and found the bag, because the Constitution prohibits only government intrusions, not family snooping. Thus, the evidence that the needle had insulin—the fateful, dispositive evidence of guilt—was allowed. Rather, the court reversed because the police (it ruled) should have obtained a search warrant before sending some of the other contents of the black bag (that is, the drugs which had but a peripheral place in the trial) for analysis.

Again, we will not explore the fine points of the Constitution because there is an overwhelming point that makes the court's holding so weak: the defense maintained throughout the trial that the black bag belonged *not* to the defendant, but to the comatose victim, Mrs. Martha von Bulow. It tried (unsuccessfully) to convince the jury that Mrs. von Bulow had injected herself with the fatal dosages. Since Claus has claimed throughout that the black bag was Martha's, how could he also claim that *his* constitutional rights had been violated when the police later sent some of its contents for chemical analysis without a search warrant? The Rhode Island Supreme Court never explains what seems to be a monumental inconsistency.

As the second (and final) act of *Glengarry Glen Ross* is about to end, Levene's guilt becomes known, and the following speech and stage direction take place (Baylen is the police officer): "Baylen [to Levene]: *Get in the goddamn room.* (Baylen starts manhandling Shelly into the room)."

That is, by far, rougher treatment than von Bulow ever received. And if *Glengarry Glen Ross* were to have an act 3, we would surely see some judge lecturing Levene sternly for his grievous misdeeds (scene 1), a fruitless appeal that is decided in minutes (scene 2), and then, as the final curtain drops, Levene languishing in prison for a year or two (scene 3).

If the Shelly Levenes of this world wised up they would take courses at Berlitz before they broke the law. Or, sadly, so it must seem to a lot of people.

June 6, 1984

A *Sign of the Times*

A federal judge, feeling bound by the recent appellate court decision in *White House Vigil v. Clark*, enjoined the public display of picture number 145 in the current Metropolitan Museum of Art exhibit, "Van Gogh in Arles." That picture, *Self-Portrait with Bandaged Ear* (oil on canvas), was painted to memorialize the artist's having cut off his right ear. Its display was enjoined because the court found it to be "unaesthetic." After careful consideration His Honor refused, however, to enjoin either number 101 (*The Nightlife Cafe*) or number 49 (*The Sower*), although he found both to be "eerie" and "too heavy on the yellow." This from a judge who thinks ecru is an accounting term.

The White House Vigil case involves complicated rules posited by the National Park Service to regulate picketing on the White House sidewalk. Most of the rules concern the safety of the president and are, of course, not at issue here. Rather, the focus is on a rule unrelated to safety, one that was drafted only "to protect the aesthetics of the White House view." It seems that the sensitive Park Service is concerned that tourists in Washington cannot always snap pictures of a completely unobstructed White House because the main gate is often clogged with pickets. Hence, the government regulation that requires those pickets to keep moving whenever they are in the "central zone," that is, within twenty yards of the front entrance. At all other White House sidewalk sites they can sit down, or stand still, or otherwise remain immobile.

The theory seems to be that tourists, if quick on the shutter button, would be able to snap an uncluttered picture of the White House through the marching protesters. Believe it or not, this petty, silly bureaucratic solution to a nonexistent problem (after all, anyone at any time can walk right up to the White House fence and take a whole roll of unobstructed pictures) was actually upheld by the Court of Appeals of the District of Columbia on lofty, aesthetic grounds.

The lower court had ruled that that regulation violated the pro-testers' constitutional right of free speech. But the appeals court (one judge dissenting) reversed, with these stirring words: "It is well-established that the government's power to regulate private

affairs encompasses the power to promote aesthetic goals." The regulation was thus upheld because many "tourists believe that the proliferation of stationary signs within the center zone sub-stantially detracts from their ability to view the White House and its grounds."

One problem with the White House Vigil decision is that every sign carried by every picket—unless made of cellophane or glass—blocks somebody's view of something. In each instance, the federal court will now have to decide whether the view being obscured was more aesthetically important than the message being conveyed. There will be thousands of such cases in a year of normal labor relations; but in the years of an automobile strike, for instance, courts would have no time for any other litigation. Some cases would be easier than others. For example, objectors frequently picket the Miss America Pageant, claiming that that extravaganza demeans women. There is no doubt that any sign that obscures a contestant—I remember, wistfully, Miss Idaho of 1977—will necessarily be enjoined as blocking the view of some-thing "aesthetically pleasing."

On the other extreme, the placards of striking miners would be blocking the view only of coal pits. Still, there might be some judges of the Realism School, judges who admired, for instance, the photographs of Dorothea Lange (have you ever seen those wonderful pictures of the Depression and the dust bowl?) who would find great dignity and beauty in the very poverty of an abandoned mine shaft. So, even Appalachian mineworkers might find their picket signs banned by the court because of overriding aesthetic considerations.

But the point of this essay is not to criticize the court but to suggest a practical compromise between protesting pickets and protesting aesthetes: On the White House side of each placard would be the message meant to stir the presidential conscience ("Save the Whale"; "Save the Snail"; "Save the Emu"; "Save the Gnu"; and by those who are not special pleaders, "Save the Zoo") or stir the presidential memory ("Remember the Maine"; this would be balanced by a counter-demonstrator carrying a banner that read "Forget Little Big Horn"; and there would be yet another poster, borne by someone who was more neutral on nostalgia: "Recalling Grenada Is Optional") or stir the president to action ("Fifty-four Forty or Fight"; "Defend Quemoy and Matsu Forever").

On the other side of each placard, the side facing the aesthetes from Toledo, there could be reproductions of famous art works; for instance, portraits by Rembrandt. In fact the Park Service could issue some of its famous regulations and require those who picket the White House to change the "other-side" art works monthly, so that frequent tourists could see, on successive trips, the French Impressionists (in May), the German Expressionists (in June), and Gilbert Stuart portraits (in July, to coincide with Independence Day celebrations). So, while the president was facing the usual battery of messages, frequent visitors to Washington, D.C., could be earning credits toward an art degree.

But what is most upsetting about the White House Vigil decision is not that there are federal judges who think that their (or the Park Service's) personal aesthetic judgments can limit the First Amendment, although that principle is plenty bad. Far worse is the fact that those judges, applying that subjective test, were able to find that a building, whether the White House or the Taj Mahal, was more beautiful than free men with strong opinions petitioning their government, peacefully.

November 19, 1984

Afterthoughts on the Goetz Case

Bernard Goetz was surrounded by a hostile group of four troublemakers on the subway, but he outgunned them all. It wasn't as daring or as romantic as it sounds, because nobody else had a gun. In the ensuing exchange of fire, one of the four was maimed for life. But Goetz survived unscathed, not even a nick, when the jury found him not guilty except on the minor, technical charge of the illegal possession of a weapon. How it can be wrong to carry a gun but okay to shoot it is a distinction that is too subtle for me to understand. But the public applauded the verdict, the politicians hedged ("I always abide by the rulings of the Court"), and the case is now history.

In thinking about the Goetz case, it wasn't only the verdict that made it so depressing and drab. The hero himself was probably the most unflamboyant marksman ever. Someone even suggested that the jury voted to acquit because sending Goetz to jail would not be real punishment, since it would change his lifestyle hardly at all. But compared to those dreary witnesses who testified at the trial every day, Mr. Goetz was almost a sparkler.

If the Goetz case was, at the same time, the year's biggest trial and the drabbest show in town, what does it take for the law to be exciting? Simple—some fiction. I didn't come upon the answer by myself. Rather, as I was thinking about Goetz I began to read *Presumed Innocent*, this season's best-selling novel about a murder and a murder trial. But unlike the transcript of the Goetz trial, the account of the trial in *Presumed Innocent* has become a Book-of-the-Month Club alternate selection. I won't give the plot away, but it involves some adultery, some police corruption, some political hokum, and a few intimacies (between the deceased divorcee and a few other characters in the book, including the judge). In other words, all it takes to make the law interesting is a little imagination, a little poetry.

Just a few changes and the Goetz case, too, would be on the *New York Times* best-seller list for weeks. Goetz himself could even stay as he is to give the story a touch of verisimilitude. But the background, the stage, would be painted in somewhat brighter, sharper hues. For instance, the train in which the incident occurs would not be pulling into the Chambers Street Station, one of the dullest subway stops in the entire system; instead it would all take place on the Lexington Avenue Express heading for Fifty-ninth Street and Bloomingdale's. Nor would the accosters be asking Goetz for $5, because $5 at Bloomingdale's is nothing. And there couldn't be a crime if all that the alleged wrongdoers wanted was nothing; let's make it $50.

The assailants would also need modification; instead of a homogeneous group of four black youths, there would be an ethnic mix (New York, after all, is the world's most famous melting pot), including an Asian seductress in a slinky low-cut dress. And instead of fleeing to Concord, New Hampshire, that most sterile of New England towns with its white church steeple, our fictionalized Mr. Goetz would hoof it to East Hampton. His confession would be taped not at a drab local police station but on the dunes before a camera crew helicoptered in from New York by a TV network for an exclusive.

But it wouldn't be all high-life and girls for the hero, who was once so meek, because the denouement would probably disappoint him: the jury would almost surely find him guilty on all counts. I've thought about this point carefully. Why would a real-life jury have freed Goetz, while the fictional panel would have given him many years in a cell? The reason says something about the law. The real jury consists of twelve people; and any result can be blamed on the need to compromise, the need to reach a consensus. No one person can be blamed if that result is wrong, or even inexplicable. But all the fictionalized jury votes are cast by just one person, the author.

Responsibility for the decision cannot be avoided. And the writer (or any person not protected by a consensus view) would, I hope, veto the presumptuous-defense principle, invoked by the real Goetz, that holds that if a wrongdoer starts something then the victim has the moral and constitutional right to finish it as violently as he wants. On the other hand, that very principle was adopted virtually unanimously by the nation at the time of Hiroshima, so in that sense it may almost be the law of the land.

This essay is getting out of hand. The Goetz case was depressing, so the muse was invoked to uplift the spirits. But instead we end up with a discussion of an atomic holocaust. Ah, for the good old days of Deuteronomy, when there was no subway crime, no nuclear deterrents, and retribution was limited ("an eye for an eye") to getting even.

August 11, 1987

V. *The Difficulty of Justice*

Time and the Law

Albert Einstein won many honors and fame for asserting, ostensibly for the first time, that Time is relative. But all that Mr. Einstein proved by his wasted efforts and formulas with funny symbols was that he was not, poor fellow, a lawyer. Time has been relative in the law for some 2,500 years. In Periclean Athens the length of speeches in court was determined by the seriousness of the case, and measured by a water-clock. Today, the only correlation between the importance of a case and the time it takes is an inverse one; the Pentagon Papers case was decided by the district court, circuit court, and U.S. Supreme Court before most of us could recover $25 for a defective model airplane.

But the purpose of this essay is not to evaluate whether the judicial system spends its time wisely or not, but to demonstrate that Time qua Time so pervades the law that not only Time but also justice is relative as a result.

The law, sadly, is like a hundred clocks, ticking, ticking, ringing, pealing. It's ten days to answer this, twenty days to answer that, thirty days to appeal, forty-five days to apply for one thing, sixty days to petition for another. And it's a statute of limitations of one year, two years, three years, six years, ten years, or twenty years, depending on the legislature's carefully considered whim.

A lawyer's main task (some say his only task) is to get more Time from his adversaries; that is why some lawyers are so well paid. If an answer is due in twenty days, a good lawyer extends the period to twenty weeks, twenty months, then twenty ad infinitums. As long as the number is still twenty, even twenty eons, the illusion is honored that the request is not dilatory. Since so much Time is spent getting more Time, there is hardly Time to do the substantive job. One expert in a timework study analysis described it as Sisyphean. The bar association angrily rejected that conclusion on the stated ground that lawyers were good family men and not promiscuous.

The law celebrates each Time of the year the way merchants

do. Stores, appropriately, have Christmas displays in December and spring displays in April. Similarly, the reasons for delay in every case are consistent with the season. In winter, a two-week adjournment is sought because there is snow and someone's train was twenty minutes late into Grand Central. In summer, a one-month postponement is requested because a secretary took a Friday afternoon off. It is a little harder with the more moderate spring and fall, but that is where good lawyers show their worth.

In rural areas, spring floods have been worth an additional four or five months; in the city, that device is good for those who use the East River Drive, or who know someone who does. Lawyers who use the subways have, however, managed. They may claim that they took the children to the stadium and the game went an extra inning, or that they planted some tomato seeds in a window box and were kept busy watching to see what happened. In the autumn one telephones one's adversary to explain that more Time is needed because, unexpectedly, the days have gotten shorter.

Time, for all its benefits of putting off forever what could be done next year, is a burden to the conscientious. The worst experience a serious lawyer has is to arrive some place more than two minutes early. "I could have made the next train so I'd not have to sit around here waiting, waiting, waiting." "I could have read almost one more page of the 1943 Revisions of 'The Newfoundland Tax Code.' Why didn't I think to bring it along?" A lawyer who once arrived at court in lower Manhattan six minutes early, unexpectedly, is rumored to have left in order to hurry back to his office on the theory he could get some work done before the gavel fell; his office was in New Rochelle.

Time has tyrannized the law from the beginning. Since Time is a function of the earth's predictable course around the sun, one practical way for lawyers to escape the clutch of Time is to hang out one's shingle on some star in the galaxy beyond the sun, where there would be no hours and no days, hence no Time. Wouldn't it be lovely to be able to fashion a wholly new system of law, based on ethics and noble thoughts, unencumbered by the constant need to respond to that petition by tomorrow or to that affidavit by the day after? And so several elegant Wall Street types took a space shuttle that was headed for Betelgeuse, intending to write Timeless Laws in the Sky, which, they noted, would be the very opposite of the Lawless Times on Earth. A few hundred light years out, with a long way still to go, they began to wonder if it was really possible to create a legal system without Time. "Probably not," opined one, "because then there would be no way to calculate whether a jail sentence was so lengthy as to be unconstitutional." Another agreed, on the ground (even though they were then 2,800 trillion miles from the ground) that without Time there would be no way of knowing whether their spaceship should be depreciated for tax purposes over five years or six.

Hearing them, the truth was out. It wasn't Time that was at fault. Indeed, the one and only inexhaustible thing in the universe is Time. No matter how much Time may be wasted, there is an infinite amount of Time left. Oxygen and land and trees may not even last this century, but Time alone is used but never spent. Nor is the law to blame, for since the days of Moses, everyone has known what is right and what is wrong. If Time is so bountiful, and Law so majestic, who is it who mixed the two so that a little old lady will be evicted onto the wintry street if she doesn't pay her rent in forty-eight hours? As with *Dred Scott* and Watergate, the LL.B.'s have been blamed.

What is obviously needed on Betelgeuse, therefore, is a legal system without lawyers. Were that so, law in that heavenly realm would be just and leisurely, and Betelgeuse would replace Belgium as the most densely populated place in the universe.

January 16, 1979

In Praise of the Tentative

The Ayatollah Khomeini sits cross-legged and metes out justice that is cross-eyed. That twisted, fearful symmetry has condemned to death heathens, heretics, pagans, infidels, and those who play, whistle, or hum Western music. The banned Western music referred to here is not the Nashville kind, which might make the ayatollah seem reasonable; it is, rather, the works of Bach, Mozart, and Beethoven. The ayatollah, as he sits in judgment, has no doubts.

The essence of our law, on the other hand, is that everything is doubtful; all is tentative; nothing is final. Cases that are lost can be appealed up and up and up until they disappear forever in the haze of the ionosphere. And if, somehow, an appeal is finally decided, the legislature may, sooner or later, reverse the court by changing the law. And sometimes, years and years later, a court may hold that an earlier opinion that had been faithfully followed a thousand times was wrongly decided in the first place. In *Erie Railroad v. Tomkins*, decided in 1938, the Supreme Court of the United States held that a decision that it itself had rendered in 1842 was not only wrong but unconstitutional. Why are the railroads always so late to arrive, even in the law?

Justice Brandeis once said that nothing is ever finally decided until it is decided justly; but since each person and each generation has his (and its) own idea of what is "just," there never can be a definitive, final decision on any ethical, social, or political issue. The law is a syllogism which seems to tail off at the conclusion into something much vaguer than any of the premises. That is due, in part, to muddled judges, who seem to think that deductive reasoning means that the issue can be ducked. It is also because whereas our social and political problems are crisp, the legal solutions, if any, are equivocal. So if nothing in the law ever seems to be finally resolved, that is how it should be, how it must be. Everyone appreciates that except litigants, who find themselves paying 120 for a perpetual-motion machine. Nothing in the law is final or irretrievable, except death. Which brings me, finally, to the purpose of this essay: to question capital punishment.

Capital punishment requires two certainties: first, the factual certainty that the defendant is the guilty party; and second, the social-political-ethical certainty that capital punishment is the proper penalty. I suggest that our experience with the ayatollah's certainties ought give us deep doubts about ever being certain enough to inflict capital punishment.

As to whether the man in the dock was the doer of the deed, errors are made more often than we dare admit. We know how unlikely it was that Nicola Sacco or Bartolomeo Vanzetti killed anyone in Braintree, Massachusetts, on April 15, 1920. A recent book suggests strongly that Bruno Richard Hauptmann did not kidnap or kill the Lindbergh baby and that there were officials in New Jersey who knew it. And one writer has argued that the government's case against Ethel Rosenberg may have been somewhat less sure than the case against her husband.

Several years ago, in Brooklyn, one George Whitmore seemed to be the murderer because a certain button was found in his possession, and the victim's coat was missing a button. The case seemed simple, except that a last-minute microscopic investigation revealed that it was a different button. How many George Whitmores have been found guilty? Just last year one Edmund Jackson was found guilty of a Queens murder; his conviction was upheld, without dissent, by both New York State appellate courts. The conviction was reversed by the federal court (per *Broderick, J.,* the former police commissioner) because defendant Jackson had been pointed out to witnesses *before* he was put into the lineup (from which he was then readily selected). It was like asking a Lilliputian to pick out which one was Gulliver.

But faulty identification is not the main reason for opposing capital punishment. Even more important is our fallible judgment. For instance, as we sputter into the 1980s our economy is *still* based on the premise that the price of oil can never exceed $4.50 a barrel. (Our government's analysis does seem unassailable: if oil were to rise to more than $4.50, users would immediately substitute coal; and if any oil producer sought to raise the price, competing producers, eager for our business, would instantly force the price back down.) Why should we think that our judgment on capital punishment is any sounder than our judgment on Arabian crude?

The factors affecting one's judgment on the issue of capital punishment are more complicated and more subtle than the pricing of oil, f.o.b. Abadan. It is doubtful, therefore, whether any political authority (the government, judge, and jury) can *always* be trusted with the power to end a life. For instance, no line can be drawn between a "pure" murder trial and a murder trial tinged with (or dominated by) political or ethnic overtones. We may be aghast because most of the 697 people (according to one count) the ayatollah has sent before his firing squad seem guilty mainly of political opposition; one victim was charged only with having supported Israel; and several appear to have been women of the evening, who granted favors, they thought, apolitically. But even in our own country, where due process is the highest, we cannot *always* disentangle the alleged murderer from his personality and beliefs; *Massachusetts v. Sacco-Vanzetti* is but the most enduring example. In other murder trials, the race or sex or beliefs or appearance, both of the defendant and the victim, are unintentional but omnipresent factors. One supposes a conviction for murder would be less likely where the accused was a white, elderly, gentle lady dressed in hand-sewn gingham (remember *Arsenic and Old Lace*), and the murdered victim an alcoholic, mean, unemployed, obese Black Panther. I think it may even be fair to say that no trial can be dispassionate where capital punishment is involved.

In short, capital punishment may be too potent a weapon for any people to have, for even we, in our country, have not *always* been able to deal with it wisely. The strongest argument in favor of electrocution is the emotional one that the murderer is the cruelest man on earth, so that his speedy loss would be our thankful gain. In Russia and China and Germany and Uganda, we note, capital punishment has been used the way we use amphetamines; pop a few and all your problems disappear. What a better world if capital punishment could be eliminated everywhere. And what better place to start, as an example, but in

America, where every known precaution is already taken to guarantee a fair trial. If even we, with all our safeguards, abolish the death sentence, it might be a faint glimmer in the long Siberian night.

January 11, 1980

Out, Damned Spot!

Marinus van der Lubbe would be alive today, if medicine were as advanced as the law. Mr. Lubbe was convicted in 1933 of setting the Reichstag fire;* a West Berlin court has now reversed that conviction on the procedural ground that the trial, conducted by Nazi judges, was unfair. Although Mr. Lubbe's good name has been retroactively restored, he is unable to savor the moment because the doctors have been unable to restore his good health; he was executed in 1934.

Physics has spent the last seventy-five years trying to understand the nature of time. But the law has gone far beyond physics; the law has *reversed* time. And the law did it without all those costly experiments involving high-energy particles and nuclear contraptions; the law did it by the simple and inexpensive technology of judicial fiat. When the West German court announced in December 1980 that Mr. Lubbe's guilt of 1933 had been magically expunged, lawyers and judges throughout the world began to apply that new Retroactive Principle to other legal problems.

The most immediate practical impact was in the family court, where petitions were filed by persons seeking to change their mates ab initio. Men who had been brooding for fifty years because they had not married that raven-haired girl next door, or the girl whose family was in the struggling new computer business, petitioned the courts for retroactive divorces and weddings. Caterers who had long gone out of business were planning menus for affairs at the Astor and the Broadway Central; and bookings were suddenly up for honeymoons on the *Queen Elizabeth* and the *Normandie*.

---

*The Reichstag fire and subsequent trial of Marinus van der Lubbe, a Dutchman, "served as a pretext (by the Nazis) for the banning of the Communist party, arrest of its members, and eventually the destruction of the free trade union movement and the non-Communist left wing" (*New York Times*, Dec. 30, 1980, p. A3).

Appointment to the bar association's Nunc Pro Tunc Committee was much more sought after than a judicial appointment, for a mere court's decision could be reversed retroactively at any time. Like the baseball Hall of Fame Committee selecting old timers, the Nunc Pro Tunc Legal Committee met to decide what old decisions should be chosen for annulment. First to go was *Marbury v. Madison,* which gave courts the power to declare acts of Congress unconstitutional. Law deans and professors argued that without *Marbury,* without judicial review, the Republic would falter. But lo and behold, *Marbury* was erased and the Constitution was, nonetheless, forever preserved and honored by the People who were not judges.

Next to be stricken was *Dred Scott;* the argument was that, since that decision was considered to be a principal cause of the Civil War, the war might be averted if the decision could be undone. And so *Dred Scott* was reversed, *nunc pro tunc.* But the Battle of Bull Run and the Battle of Gettysburg were fought right on schedule. An awful truth began to emerge: the law didn't affect anything. Two of the most historic decisions ever rendered were blithely nullified, and nothing was changed except a few law textbooks.

An attempt was made to undo *Brown v. Board of Education,* and the Ford Foundation commissioned several studies to investigate what would have happened to students of all races had *Brown* never been decided. But before those sociological analyses could be completed, old Mr. Ford seized the moment and eliminated the Ford Foundation ab initio. And gone forever was the world's largest hoard of charts and graphs. Gone too, noted Mr. Ford with a twinkle, was the Edsel.

One wonders why it took the German court until December 1980 to undo the trial of Mr. Lubbe, since the whole world knew the truth in 1933. My college textbook *This Age of Conflict,* written in 1943, attributed Lubbe's conviction not to any evidence but to Herr Goering's "flash of intuition." And William L. Shirer, in *The Rise and Fall of the Third Reich* (1959) wrote (p. 268): "there is enough evidence to establish beyond a reasonable doubt that it was the Nazis who planned the arson and carried it out for their own political ends."

But the half-century delay in admitting the truth is not the main objection to the reversal; rather, the reversal itself is wrong. For the court seems to feel that, since that particular wrong has now been undone, German law in the period 1933–1945 has been absolved. Hans Frank, the Nazi governor of Poland, said it better just before he was hanged at Nuremberg: "A thousand years will pass and the guilt of Germany will not be erased."

How Macbeth and Lady Macbeth wished that they could have undone their frightful deeds. For Macbeth knew that he "shall sleep no more" (act 2, scene 2) and wished he had "but died an hour before this chance" (act 2, scene 3). And Lady Macbeth cried as she wandered in the fitful night: "Out, damned spot. Out, I say" (act 5, scene 1).

Mr. Lubbe's trial is a stain that will never wash. And that trial is symbolic of a time and place in history that will never, never, never wash. But there are people always trying to convince the world, or maybe just themselves, that nothing happened in Germany that can't be undone.

The British government's Royal Eternal Review Commission saw a way out of England's financial crisis. Parliament simply rescinded the Stamp Act and the Quartering Act, *nunc pro tunc*, and so the American Revolution never took place. That did have important consequences. It precipitated the biggest recall in the history of the Department of Transportation. Some 97 million registered cars and trucks, built after the 1776 model year, had to have their steering wheels moved to the right-hand side. No one knows how Rolls Royce, thought to be so careful, could have made such an error.

Seeing all those Silver Clouds in the repair shop started people thinking that maybe the law was wrong, and maybe Lady Macbeth was right: "What's done cannot be undone" (act 5, scene 1).

January 26, 1981

Ode to the Good Ol' Days

In Keats's immortal poem, *Ode on a Grecian Urn,* he describes two lovers etched in pottery, frozen in time; despite their 3,000-year ardor, they have yet to kiss. In Sidney Zion's essays, which are not immortal (*Read All About It,* Summit Books, 1982), the journalist-lawyer tries to freeze the law as it was twenty years ago when Earl Warren was the Chief and the good guys formed the High Court's majority. But in the law, as in love, not even yesterday can be held over.

It would be nice, of course, to do as Mr. Zion has done, as if the law were based on astrology. Just pick some auspicious past moment when the planets were happily aligned and declare that that is the preordained moment of truth. If the laws could be frozen as of 1802, before the Louisiana Purchase added Gulf Coast floods and a lot of Republican electoral votes to the nation, President Carter would have been reelected and the Dodgers would still be in Brooklyn. There would be no income tax and no nuclear waste. And it would be nice, too, having Thomas Jefferson as president; somehow money would then be found to support the arts without canceling one frigate from the defense budget.

While Whigs and Aquarians might prefer 1802, abstainers and Scorpios would have a different choice. The Women's Temperance League, scotching rumors that it had disappeared forever into the foggy Irish Mist would, with wry humor, campaign to establish the year 1920, the first full year of Prohibition, as our nation's governing date. And every other special-interest group would have its own special year with its own special proposal. Bigots would want to freeze the law as it was before *Brown v. Board of Education* (1954); sexists, a hardy breed, would argue for a time prior to the Women's Suffrage (Nineteenth) Amendment; nudists would want to go back to the idyllic days of Adam and Eve; some economists (rumored to be stubborn remnants from the Roosevelt administration) would want the governing laws to predate the law of supply and demand; and people without garages would be happy to return to the days before there were regulations imposing alternate street parking. But most citizens, if given a choice, would accept the law just as it is now, confiscatory tax rates and all; for there doesn't really seem to be any practical alternative.

This piece is prompted by the publication of Mr. Zion's essays. He reports, breathlessly and in staccato prose (as if it were red-hot news), that the Burger Court's views on the criminal law differed decisively from the views expounded by the Court under Chief Justice Warren. His plan is to return the law to its pristine form of the 1960s. Ah! Those were the days! The point of this essay is not to quarrel with Mr. Zion's irrefutable conclusion that the criminal-defense bar (and the felonious rascals themselves) miss the Ol' Warren Court, but to put that conclusion in context.

Putting Mr. Zion in context is just a polite way of putting him down. For the crux of the matter is that his essays on the law are irreconcilable. He lavishly praises the Warren Court for "making its revolution in criminal procedure" and "expand[ing] civil liberties to a degree that had never before been approached." But because the Burger Court has retreated on those same issues, Mr. Zion accuses it of "violating wholesale the Bill of Rights." The point is this: since those pined-for rights did not even exist until the 1960s, their disappearance in the 1970s and 1980s cannot fairly be described as a desecration of the Constitution. I hasten to add that I, too, much prefer Mr. Warren's rulings to Mr. Burger's. But, sad to admit, even that doesn't make the one right and the other unconstitutional.

And sometimes, although it is as infrequent as Halley's Comet, the Burger Court may not even be wrong. (N.B. I didn't say that it was right; I've too many friendships at stake for that.) Take, for instance, the case of *Scheckloth v. Bustamonte*, the subject of one of Mr. Zion's angriest pieces: It was 2:40 A.M. in Sunnyvale, California, and police officers on routine traffic patrol flagged down a car that had a broken headlight and broken license-plate light. The driver (through no fault of the cops; no torture was alleged) did not have his license. Nor did anyone else in the car (there were five passengers) seem to have registration papers, although one occupant claimed that the car belonged to his brother.

After the six men had alighted from the car, one of the officers asked in a routine way whether the vehicle could be searched. The man claiming to be the owner's brother not only said, "Sure, go ahead" (an exact quote) but immediately opened the trunk and the glove compartment on his own. The police, realizing that they'd not find much in either the trunk or glove compartment, reached under a seat and there chanced upon stolen checks.

The only question before the Supreme Court was this: had consent for the search been given voluntarily? The majority (per Justice Stewart) held it had been; the dissenters argued otherwise, on the ground that the police had not first formally advised the six men that they could refuse. A nice point of law, and solid grist for both law reviews and psychology journals: can anyone, even one's girlfriend, give a meaningful, constitutional consent at 2:40 A.M.? But back to Sunnyvale: These six chaps were in a quandary because they were hiding contraband. Had they not consented to a search they would have betrayed their guilt. Rather than risk that, they chose to take a careful, calculated long-shot gamble and quickly and shrewdly open the doors to empty places. Their gamble lost. It is not so clear, however, that the Fourth Amendment's protection against illegal search and seizure was meant to apply to valiant men who try, but fail, to pick an inside straight.

But even if the Burger Court is not as fossilized as Mr. Zion thinks, everyone has a nostalgia for some romantic time past when things were always better, when, as Keats described it, boughs never shed their leaves. I would suggest (and here I'm probably in the minority) a return to the era of the Vinson Court.

When Fred M. Vinson was chief justice of the United States, Harry S. Truman was president; Pee Wee, Jackie, and the Duke were invincible in Brooklyn; and (this is the real point, the crux of the matter) I was a whole lot younger.

December 13, 1982

Sizing Up the Law

The *Ox-Bow Incident* (a great classic) and *The Lawyer's Almanac 1882–83* (a great drudge) are, inadvertently, variations on the same theme: the lack of individuality in the law. But the books are spiritual opposites, for in the *Ox-Bow* the lack of individuality begets tragedy; in the *Almanac*, bigness—paunchiness for paunchiness's sake—is celebrated.

The *Almanac* (crisply subtitled *A Cornucopia of Information about Law, Lawyers, and the Profession*) is, in substantial part, a book of boring irrelevancies. Of course, all statistical books necessarily include some data of waning significance. *The Encyclopedia of Baseball*, for instance, records not only Babe Ruth's home runs (714), and Henry Aaron's (745), but Pete Coscarart's (28); he was the impeccable Dodger second-baseman of my childhood. And the *World Almanac* lists not only the two longest rivers (the Nile, 4,182 miles; the Amazon, 3,912 miles), but the fiftieth (the Sungari, 1,215 miles). *The Lawyer's Almanac* has, then, this distinction: it may be the only statistical book that includes *only* irrelevancies. That itself, of course, might be a record-setting first.

The main point of the *Almanac* seems to be to record lists of the "largests" in the law, as if there were some remote, flickering connection between the bigness that it details and what the law is. It lists, by size, the largest two hundred law firms in the country. Baker and McKenzie, based in Chicago, is the China of law firms, having a total of 583 lawyers; partnership meetings are held in Comiskey Park and are necessarily scheduled only when the White Sox are on the road. There is a dead-heat among five firms for last place on the list, down there with the struggling Mets and Cincinnati Reds; they each have only 82 lawyers, 501 behind the league leaders with the season almost gone.

The *Almanac* proudly lists the twenty-five largest firms in Washington, D.C. (Covington and Burling, which has only 204 lawyers, and is ranked only twenty-eighth nationally, leads this minor league); there is a list of the twenty largest branch offices in

Washington (a Dallas firm leads the field with 89 lawyers); there is a list entitled "Fast Growing Branch Offices in Washington" (an Omaha firm showed the largest one-year gain, 83.3 percent, going from 12 to 22 lawyers; the Cleveland firm of Jones, Day, Reavis, and Pogue was the slowest of the fast growers, showing an increase of only 20.8 percent, which was, as a concerned partner has noted, still ahead of the rate of inflation); there is a list of the fifty largest corporate law departments (AT&T leads with 895 lawyers despite a decline from last year's topper of 924; if the decline continues, experts expect the company to seek relief from local utility commissions); there is a list of the ten largest trade association legal departments (led by the American Council of Life Insurance, with a staff of 26; but that's only 1 lawyer per 10 million Americans, actuarially speaking); there is a list of the ten largest annual legal fees paid by electric utilities, led by $2,065,909; and there are more lists still, but I think you get the idea.

The largest law-enforcement group in the year 1885 was the twenty-eight-man contingent that rode into the Sierra Nevadas, headed toward the Ox-Bow. They rode to redress a murder and cattle rustling. One man knew the lynch party was wrong: "'Oh, men,' he cried out, coming back at us, 'think, won't you; think.'"

But the other twenty-seven were not capable of individual thought, each man afraid to disagree with the rest: "Why are we riding up here, twenty-eight of us . . . when every one of us would rather be doing something else? . . . We're doing it because we're in the pack, because we're afraid not to be in the pack . . . we don't dare resist the pack" (Walter Van Tilburg Clark, *The Ox-Bow Incident*, 1940; New American Library edition, pp. 37 and 106).

This is not to suggest, of course, that large law firms go galloping around Foley Square out of control. But the fact is that 583 people cannot think as independently, or originally, or irreverently as can one solitary, brooding person. I know, too, that this may all be sour grapes, because twice in my life I sought to be employed by the very large firms and dispatched hundreds of résumés without luck.

But the more I consider it, the more it seems that size and the law are inversely related, and that books like *The Lawyer's Alma-*

nac border on the silly. Can you imagine a guide to English literature that listed, in order, the two hundred longest poems, the one hundred longest essays, and the fifty longest plays? Or a book on art that listed the world's largest paintings? Were that so, artists eager for recognition would petition for the exclusive right to paint one large mural that would cover the Great Wall of China; and the *Mona Lisa* (30 inches by 21 inches) would be unhooked and stored in the Louvre's sub-basement.

But, as noted, this is probably all borne of my own still bitter experience of rejection. It might be nice now, I suppose, to go to those country-club office outings every June, represent my firm at softball, and keep my opinions to myself.

September 13, 1982

"We do not understand how one could ask for a more probable danger, unless we must await till the actual eve of hostilities."

The similarities among the Affairs Valladares, Astyanax, and *Dennis*—each involved immediate punishment for but a potential wrong and, in each, the full fury of the state was focused on a fragile subject—may pose an embarrassing problem for Cuba. For in meting out justice to Señor Valladares, Premier Castro was following Western tradition and American precedent. Does not such blind adherence to Yankee ways mean that Castro himself may be a latent danger to the Cuban government, that is, that he himself may be a potential counter-revolutionary?

February 3, 1983

Some Thoughts of Liam O'Flaherty

Liam O'Flaherty, the wonderful Irish writer, died on September 7 at the age of eighty-eight in Dublin. But Frankie McPhillip, Gypo Nolan, Commander Dan Gallagher, and the other revolutionary characters who inhabit *The Informer* (1926), his most enduring novel, still live hauntingly on.

I had much sympathy for each and every one of them when I first read the book, during high school. The crowded Dublin scene described by O'Flaherty seemed so much like earlier descriptions of the Lower East Side, when people did not know whether to fight the Establishment or to emulate it. The characters from *The Informer* were not only anti-Establishment, which endeared them to all teenagers, but they were also, of course, anti-British.

When I was growing up, the British were using force to prevent the Holocaust remnants from reaching the refuge of Palestine, so being anti-British was considered, in my home, to be almost noble. While I was critical of Frankie McPhillip for shooting an official (as *The Informer* begins he is in hiding), I did distinguish then (more than I do now) between murder for political ends (wrong, but with an explanation) and murder for greed. Even Gypo Nolan, the informer, wasn't all bad. He had acted on the spur, not out of malice. And he had not spent the twenty pounds reward on pompous political tracts or other serious things, but it was all promptly dissipated in the bars and brothels of Dublin. To me, then a high school sophomore or junior, those seemed to be ideal expenditures.

Even the moralists could like *The Informer* because justice was done. McPhillip, the murderer, was himself killed by the police; and Nolan, the informer, was shot by the Organization. Of course, to be perfectly moral, the cycle of death would have to continue, with someone shooting the man who killed Nolan, ad infinitum. But more of that later.

But the contemporary scene seems less romantic. A present-day Frankie McPhillip would be Dominic McGlinchey, defendant in *McGlinchey v. Wren* (Supreme Court of Ireland, 1982, No. 149). It is an obscure and routine case because by now another murder is but routine. All we know about the defendant from the Court's opinion (per O'Higgins, Chief Justice) is his deed: he was accused of murdering "an elderly grandmother" who had been "riddled with bullets." There was no denial; only the explanation, for what it's worth, that it was all done for the cause of Ireland.

The narrow legal question before the Court was whether McGlinchey should be extradited to Northern Ireland, the scene of his alleged activities. There was a nice legal point involved because the Extradition Act specifically exempts "a political offense." But the chief justice put that defense aside abruptly, holding that "modern terrorist violence was the antithesis of what could reasonably be regarded as political."

And so, while McGlinchey was promptly extradited, we do not know the answers to any of the really interesting questions: Who was the murdered grandmother? Why was she chosen? Was it at random, or had she harbored Protestant militiamen? Had she opposed Irish unity or was her family active in the British cause? Or, worst of all, had she been an informer? Liam O'Flaherty wrote a whole book on these points but the Court, of course, just takes the facts as it finds them. The law, unlike the novel, is not interested in the tableau.

When you read of the Dominic McGlincheys you begin to wonder whether or not Frankie McPhillip, and all the Frankie McPhillips since the 1920s, have not died in vain. Underscoring the connection between the 1920s and now, we note this incidental historical fact: Chief Justice O'Higgins's uncle, Kevin O'Higgins, a minister in the Free State government, was himself murdered in 1927. I think it would be hard, were O'Flaherty to have written his novel in the 1980s, to have made his characters so likeable.

But if the law, by its nature, doesn't reach beyond the surface, reaching is the very business of the novel. The most provocative character in *The Informer* is a minor one, Mary McPhillip, sister of the dead Frankie. Commander Dan Gallagher tells her, "We have discovered the informer, Mary. Your brother will be shortly avenged. It was Gypo Nolan who betrayed him."

She replies, "You're not going to kill him. That would only be another murder. It wouldn't help the dead. Lord have mercy on him."

And as the book ends, even Mrs. McPhillip, the dead man's mother, expresses a softer view. She tells the dying Gypo Nolan, "I forgive ye. Ye didn't know what ye were doing."

When I first read *The Informer*, a long time ago, I thought that O'Flaherty was not only a novelist but something of a prophet, urging forgiveness and reconciliation as the only way to end the cycle of death. It was easy to think that, because all of the characters in *The Informer* were likeable, even, almost, Frankie McPhillip himself. But now, when confronted by the McGlincheys of the world, it seems that such a notion is romantic and naive. It has been apparent for a long time that the law has no solution for ideological murder, no way to cope. It is disquieting to think that the matter may be beyond even the reach of a great novelist.

September 26, 1984

Achilles' Shield, and Ours

The *Wall Street Journal*, which daily dispatches itself around the world via the bargain, subsidized second-class mail rate, thinks that everyone else should pay his own way. And so a recent *Journal* editorial bemoaned that a litigant could begin an endless lawsuit in federal court by paying only a "paltry" $60 filing fee, a fee that, according to the *Journal*'s analysis, covered only 2 percent of the government's cost.

Inspired by that editorial, the Accountants (always a bit jealous of lawyers) realized that only drastic action could balance the budget and save the Republic from fiscal ruin. And one night soon thereafter, at precisely one second past 11 P.M. (so as to take advantage of the very lowest telephone rates) the Accountants staged a coup d'etat. In keeping with the ancient traditions of their craft, it was neatly done, bloodless, and humorless. All key government buildings were secured before dawn by pith-helmeted CPAs, armed with sharpened red, white, and blue ballpoints. A reassuring message was read to the nation at 7:59 A.M. (while the night rates were still in effect) in which the Head Accountant asked the people to stay calm, and promised a return to a freely elected profligate civilian government as soon as the budget was balanced.

A few fiscal reforms, which were not controversial and could be readily implemented, were to be put into effect at once: since so many Supreme Court decisions were 5–4, it meant that eight justices, and their clerks and staffs, were mere supernumeraries; they could be discharged without impairing the judicial process. Labor negotiations were going on at that very moment to see which justice would work for the lowest wage (although the Accountants had pledged not to violate the $3.35 per hour minimum set by a previous Congress). A similar plan would pare the Congress where 200 senators and 435 representatives all did the exact same duplicatory work of holding hearings and passing *139* laws. Ninety-nine senators and 434 congressmen were mere extras, bloating the budget and our taxes.

And there were other obvious economies that would save additional millions, or was it billions, or maybe trillions each and every year. For instance, a costly analysis revealed that all government departments, except the Treasury, operated at a loss. And so the departments of State, Labor, Agriculture, Defense, Education, Commerce, Justice, and Energy were padlocked that afternoon. The projected benefits totaled $698 billion, or was it $986 trillion.

The second stage of the Revolution involved more complicated cost accounting. The filing fee in federal court was raised from $60 to $3,000; since the $60 represented only 2 percent of costs, that was easy to calculate. It also meant that, with fewer cases, one Supreme Court justice could be part-time, thereby saving the health benefits that were paid to full-time employees only.

Other cost allocations were more difficult. For instance, since much of the government's historic purpose was to protect free speech under the First Amendment, each citizen would be issued a metering device that would count the number of words spoken each month, and the speaker would be billed accordingly. It was cumbersome, but it was fair; otherwise some Harpo Marx and some Edward I. Koch would be paying the same tax.

Despite the menacing presence of those ballpoint-bearers, came the thermidor. It began when a few of the bravest of the brave suggested, in an unsigned samizdat pamphlet, that a balanced budget was not greater than the Magna Carta. Others noted, in hushed whispers, that the rights to unlimited litigation and unlimited speech were basic to a free society; the Russians had neither. Then a classicist explained that the lawsuit was, to the ancient Greeks, a symbol of peace and democracy. When the great Achilles decided to rejoin the battle for Troy (*The Iliad*, book 18) his new shield was forged by Hephaistos, said to be the son of Zeus and Hera. That "huge and heavy shield" depicted, symbolically, both scenes of war (a city under siege) and scenes of peace (a trial before judges). Thus, at least since Homer's time, Western culture has considered the lawsuit as the free man's alternative to fighting.

With that new and profound perspective, the Accountants' Revolution just melted away. Quietly, the speech-metering devices were disconnected; and quietly, employees of all ranks, from cabinet officers to typists, began to drift back to the huge buildings that had been standing empty on Constitution Avenue. And if the great wheels of justice could be turned on by an aggrieved citizen for a "paltry" $60, that was as wonderful a story as any that Homer ever told.

June 24, 1985

VI. *Law School*

Thoughts Prompted by a Book Review

Partly because the Law School library was so crowded, partly because the lighting there was so bad, and partly because there was just too much chit-chat (of which I was more guilty than most), I decided to study in the university's main library.

As I wandered about the Sterling Library, looking for a quiet niche, I came across a room with a sign that announced that no women were allowed. Since Yale in those days had no women undergraduates and rather few women throughout—the Law School had but a smattering—I was curious about a room that would be so chaste. But it was wonderfully comfortable, much like the Union League Club depicted in *New Yorker* cartoons, with big leather chairs. I settled into one of them, in a quiet alcove, and knowing that I'd not be disturbed I began to underline my various law school casebooks. It was wearisome stuff, not nearly as interesting as college, but I was nothing if not dutiful. When I needed a break, I just reached for the books in front of me; I was in a section devoted to the British poets of World War I.

At first, I read casually, and then with more care, the three poets whose works chanced to be right there, Rupert Brooke, Wilfred Owen, and Isaac Rosenberg. All three had died in the war, and they were grouped on the same shelf as if in a common literary grave. It was morose, but it helped to put things in perspective, for here were three men of genius who had died at about my age and here was I, at Yale, in a big leather chair.

I studied at that same spot, in that same seat, often during the rest of my law school days. If someone was already in my place, I waited and fidgeted in another, but it was never for too long, because undergraduates in those days did not have much staying power.

Those three dead war poets raised serious questions for me as I underlined more and more casebooks on subjects that seemed more and more remote from the things that really seemed to mat- *145* ter, remote from the flowers that grew in the beautiful, small inner courtyard just outside my favorite library room. For what was the law if these three good men, each more talented than all of us at the Law School put together, could die so young without any law having been violated? They hadn't broken any law when they lived, and their deaths were in accordance with all the rules. I thought, too, how empty those deaths had been because World War I had not involved a lot of good people fighting a lot of evil people; it involved only a lot of dead people. I have always remembered a statistic from an undergraduate course in Modern European History (History 119–120 at Brown)—at the Battle of the Somme the British had a cannon every six yards. Since the war was a stand-off, I assumed that the Germans had the same. That was a lot of legal killing, especially for a war that had no cause.

Isaac Rosenberg wrote, in *On Receiving News of the War:*

> O' ancient crimson curse!
> Corrode, consume.
> Give back this universe
> Its pristine bloom.

I wondered in law school, as I read the poetry and the legal texts, and I wonder still, what the law does to give back the pristine bloom.

Several years ago, feeling nostalgic about my law school years, but a bit down on the law, I purchased *The Collected Poems of Rupert Brooke* and *The Collected Works of Isaac Rosenberg.* I dip into them on occasion, but the sharpness has faded. What has brought it all back to mind, and has evoked this essay, is a review in a recent (February 10, 1984) *Times Literary Supplement* of a small volume, *The Complete Poems of Wilfred Owen.* As I read that review, I thought of how, since Owen's death in 1918, the law has churned out tens of thousands of volumes of judicial opinions, tens of thousands of volumes of legislative debate, and tens of thousands of volumes of law review and other learned commentary. My guess is that Owen's one volume of anti-war poetry

("I am the enemy you killed, my friend") is the more relevant, and will last longer.

It's funny how poor lighting in the library can make the law so clear.

March 5, 1984

Professor James Remembered

The winter issue of the *Yale Law Report* brought the sad news that Professor Fleming James, Jr., had died. I had him for Procedure I and Torts II, but a particularly vivid recollection of him comes from a special research project. He remembered me not at all. I would greet him whenever I saw him at a Law School function, but he was never quite able to place me. Thinking of the impression that I must have made on him, I'm not surprised.

I was on a scholarship at the Law School and applied to do research to earn some money. Professor James hired me from the list. He explained that he needed legal research in the area of Guest Statutes; Guest Statutes, enacted in most states and in several Canadian provinces—the Saskatchewan statute was considered to be the model—defined the duty owed by the driver to someone who was a guest in his car.

The law, in its quest for infinite variety, had (and has) different sets of rules for a driver vis-à-vis (i) a guest, (ii) a passenger for hire, (iii) another driver, (iv) a pedestrian, and (v) a family member. Some have thought it harmful to let husbands and wives sue each other over automobile injuries, because a trial on whether or not the car was going too fast (or whether the driver was listening to a ballgame and was, therefore, inattentive) has, on occasion, led to harsh words and divorce; such familial litigation has also led, say the insurance companies, to exaggerated claims.

At the professor's suggestion I began my study by reading the relevant sections of *Blashfield on Automobile Law*, a seventeen-volume treatise devoted exclusively to the car's relation to the law. I would have thought that either the light was red or it was green, and that seventeen volumes was a bit extensive for so puny a topic. But the law is nothing if not an infinite variety of permutations on everything.

As for Guest Statutes, I read, of course, every relevant case cited in *Blashfield*, and then every case cited by those cases, ad infinitum. When I wrote up my topics, I furnished the professor

with scores of citations for each point, whether large or incidental. For historical background, and to display some learning (and
to show that my pay was well earned), I cited several very old
English cases; English cases were then cited (and maybe still are)
by reference to both the calendar year and the year of the sovereign's reign. I do not remember the precise case now, but I referred to a venerable decision both by its calendar year (I think it
was 1705) and as the fifth year of Queen Anne's reign. I was, I
learned, off by a year. I had cited over a hundred cases, but Professor James spotted the error instantaneously: "1705 is the fourth
year, so one of your dates is wrong."

When he peered over his glasses and asked if he wasn't right, I
confessed that I had not heard of Queen Anne until that very
citation. I explained that I had grown up in Brooklyn where we
took our hostility to George III and British royalty seriously; the
only monarch I knew of (in addition to Tyrant George) was Queen
Elizabeth, although I had seen a Charles Laughton movie about
Henry VIII. He asked, most gently, if I hadn't heard of Queen
Anne furniture, Queen Anne's lace, or Queen Anne's War. I assured him that none registered the slightest recognition.

As we chatted, he told me he had been born in China and had
grown up in New Jersey. As a boy, he had often traveled to New
York on the Dyckman Street Ferry before the George Washington
Bridge was built. I replied that I had never heard of Dyckman
Street, had never been on the George Washington Bridge, and in
fact, had never been in New Jersey. I could see by his expression
that he was no longer surprised that I had not heard of Queen
Anne (1702–1714).

One topic, on rainy law school afternoons, was which professor
was the most brilliant. It was a time—it must have been long
ago—when students actually thought the faculty wise. Although I
sometimes nominated Professor James, others (who didn't know
the Royal House of Stuart from a royal flush) argued that one
could not compare a mere torts teacher with someone who taught
jurisprudence or constitutional theory or comparative law. That
logic was, I protested, an a priori test. I didn't know exactly what it
meant then, and I'm not sure I know now, but it always won a
convert or two to my nominee.

Thinking back over all these years, as obituaries make one do, I wonder if I might not have overreacted to the Queen Anne incident. I have always been unduly impressed—almost intimidated—by people who can recite long lists and dates of anything. For instance, I remember feeling inadequate in elementary school because some kids I thought were rather ordinary could rattle off the names of all the presidents (including such unlikely ones as Rutherford Hayes and Chester Arthur) and their dates of office. I would falter after James Madison and not be able to resume until T. Woodrow Wilson; I have always been proud that I've known that Woodrow Wilson's first name was "Thomas."

Still thinking back to law school, I guess I have grown quite worldly over the years. I've moved from Brooklyn to Manhattan; our dining-room table has Queen Anne legs; I've photographed Queen Anne's lace (it's a wildflower, not a shawl or a doily); and since my mother-in-law lives in Leonia and my Sunday morning tennis game is in Englewood, I now visit New Jersey at least twice a week (and via the George Washington Bridge). I can only conclude that the practice of law must be very broadening.

May 28, 1982

About a Dreamer

Allard Kenneth Lowenstein was a perpetual-motion machine for good causes in the 1950s, 1960s, and 1970s. He'd be going nonstop still, but he was assassinated in March 1980 by a deranged young man who was once his student and his protégé.

I first met—and heard of—Al Lowenstein during our first week at Yale Law School. He came by looking for my roommate, a friend (Al explained) from Horace Mann High School. But David was home in Wilton, Connecticut, that afternoon, so Al fidgeted a bit, then put a request to me: He did not yet have a telephone and wondered if he could use our number until his was connected. Without a thought I said, "Sure"; and within seconds the thing began to ring.

The incident was not a total loss, for I learned, quite unexpectedly, some of the finer points of Einsteinian astronomy. I learned, for instance, that when it was between midnight and 8 A.M. at longitude 73 degrees West, latitude 41 degrees 43 minutes North (that is, New Haven, Connecticut), it was telephone-dialing time somewhere on this round and rotating planet of ours. It did not make it easier, especially after the novelty wore off, that the caller was Adlai Stevenson or Hubert Humphrey.

Lowenstein counseled with those kinds of folks for the rest of his life. He was adviser to Eleanor Roosevelt, Senator Frank Graham, Norman Thomas, and Martin Luther King, Jr.; he was the architect of the 1964 Mississippi Summer Project and a founder of the Mississippi Freedom Democratic party (which ran Aaron Henry, a black, for governor); his work against apartheid in South Africa and against South Africa's cruel mandate in South West Africa (now Namibia) earned him a special hearing before the United Nations; he was the moving force behind the "Dump Johnson" movement, which forced the president of the United States to retire, and helped to end the Viet Nam War; he induced Senator Eugene McCarthy to run for president; he was a congressman from New York's Fifth Congressional District (although

Governor Rockefeller prevented his reelection by some crude gerrymandering); he had several unsuccessful runs at other congressional seats, and two runs at a U.S. Senate seat (from New York) that faded early; he organized the campaign for William Fitts Ryan to run unsuccessfully for mayor of New York; he was a vital link between democrats in Spain and anti-Franco forces elsewhere (and played a role in the events that ousted the Fascists); he had ambassadorial rank at the UN. And, incredibly, much more. But I'm going to stop, for in just the recounting of it it is hard not to cry.

What prompts this essay is that David Harris has written a book, *Dreams Die Hard* (St. Martins/Marek Press, 1982), purportedly about Al, Dennis Sweeney (Al's murderer), and himself, and how they spent (or misspent) the 1960s. I say "purportedly" because the book is really about a ubiquitous ghost, with long ears and a sharp tongue. This wraith had a narrow specialization; he was always the only witness present when negative things were happening to, or said about, Al Lowenstein.

Thus, although not formally invited to Al's wedding, the apparition duly reported this about Norman Thomas: "At the luncheon, one of the bride's party gagged noticeably when the octogenarian socialist was pointed out to her" (p. 157).

We note that Mr. Norman Thomas (Princeton '05, Union Theological Seminary '11) was one of the most courtly gentlemen in America, and everybody everywhere was always delighted to meet him. As a point of personal privilege, I was at that wedding and can report that Mr. Thomas was, as always, his gracious self.

In describing the New Hampshire primary victory of Senator McCarthy, engineered by Al, the ghost alone overheard negatives and filed this dissenting report:

> When McCarthy came in, the crowd cut loose. He moved along the stage, shaking hands and exchanging greetings with most of the dignitaries, but his mood stiffened when he reached Lowenstein.
>
> "Huh," he reportedly said with a tone of suspicion, "Lowenstein. Where were you in New Hampshire?" [P. 229]

Mrs. Helen Suzman was a champion of black rights in the Union of South Africa and was one of Al Lowenstein's close friends. But our spook overheard—no one knows where—precisely when Mrs. Suzman "had finally 'had it' with Lowenstein" (p. 141).

And when the puff was on vacation, the corporeal Mr. David Victor Harris (as he usually stiffly and formally refers to himself) did the job by himself: "Allard Lowenstein's act seemed to be wearing thin that Spring" (p. 177). "He treated you as an equal until you then indeed became an equal, then he treated you as an underling or banished you to Siberia, froze you out" (p. 217).

But I really knew just from the title, *Dreams Die Hard*, that the book could not be about Al, because he never, ever, gave up on any dream. He really thought that if everyone had the right to vote, Utopia would follow within thirty days; experienced as he was in the ways of government, he always allowed for some bureaucratic lag. He was (unlike the Harris and Sweeney of the book) witty and charming, and never thought (as did Harris and Sweeney) that he was always morally perfect. Al Lowenstein was, I suppose, one of the very few original, non-Xeroxable characters of recent political life. Well, I guess that it's not entirely true that he couldn't be duplicated, because I impersonated him once myself. It was in the second week of law school. I telephoned the Southern New England Telephone Company, put my handkerchief over the speaker (a precaution that was unnecessary) and said to the operator, rather belligerently: "This is Allard K. Lowenstein. L-O-W-E-N-S-T-E-I-N. I'm over at the Yale Law School. When are you going to connect my damn phone?"

July 29, 1982

Yalelawschool
A Primitive Culture Discovered

Professor Ruth Benedict of Columbia University, in her classic text on anthropology, *Patterns of Culture*, defined "primitive" as follows: "Primitive man never looked out over the world and saw 'mankind' as a group and felt his common cause with a species. . . . His own group, and all its ways of behaving, was unique."

The book describes her visits to three ethnocentric (hence, by her definition, primitive) tribes: The Zuni of New Mexico, the Dobu of New Guinea, and the Kwakiutl of the Canadian Pacific Coast.

She need not have traveled so far, for the most ethnocentric, the most primitive tribe of all, Yalelawschool, dwells only seventy-five miles north of New York City, as the sacred crow flies. What has focused anthropological attention on this heretofore unobserved group of faculty and students is the recent statement by its new shaman, Dean-elect Guido Calabresi: "Yale Law School is the only school going where someone has the chance to be serious about legal thought but in a way that can still influence the real world."

According to the *New York Times* story, this Chief Medicine Man himself attended Yalelawschool, and before that, Yalecollege. Since he has never been off the reservation, it is not surprising that he is unaware that beyond his elegant Gothic hut there are other tribes with other headdresses, other war paint.

Scholars, who now believe that the Yalelawschool tribe is descended from the Zuni, are puzzled how such a small, self-centered, and odd community could have become so separated from its New Mexican ancestors. According to one legend, handed down through the ages as part of a ceremonial rain dance, several of the bravest Zuni of long, long ago set out to the East to find the exact place where the great sun rose, and they didn't stop until they reached the Atlantic Ocean. Since they had spent several years on their trek, and were still no nearer a solution than when they had first begun, they agreed that the omens were propitious for starting a law school.

This version is vigorously disputed by the sorcerers at Yalelawschool, who chant, through their bear masks, that the Zuni pedestrian traffic went the other way. According to their holy texts, all the Zuni lived in a sacred corner of New Haven when the world began. But thousands of years ago, before the great rivers flowed, some brave lawschool graduates, who disdained Wall Street and were eager to practice in the sun belt, set out to travel ever westward to find the exact place where the great sun set. When their scouts reported that Los Angeles law firms were no different from New York's, they stopped just where they were, and that chanced to be New Mexico. The New Haven Zuni still believe that everything in the known world originated with Yalethisorthat.

But however it all began, long ago, before the great ice melted and the oceans were formed, these two primitive Zuni communities, now separated by a continent, offer a fascinating study in similarities and contrasts. Their similarity is in their ritual, for each is still governed by what Professor Benedict called "unintelligible formulas," those magic incantations meant to placate the gods and judges.

On the fundamentals of life, though, the two Zuni tribes have grown so far apart as to be opposites. The New Mexican Zuni are Apollonian and believe in the oneness of nature. Life and death are part of the same natural cycle, a process that envelops all people and all things, great and small. The New Mexican Zuni no longer worship the sun, for they no longer worry where it rises or where it sets. They are serene and are at peace with everyone and everything.

In contrast, the New Haven Zuni are now the very opposite. They are fiercely competitive, fiercely individualistic, fiercely Dionysian. They worship the sun as fervently as they have since before the first eagle soared, since before the first environmental lawsuit was filed, because they still believe that the sun rises and sets on them alone.

March 15, 1985

Form and Substance

If lawyers are to be made like cookies, should they be chocolate chip or oatmeal raisin?

A most distressing article, "A New Design for a New Kind of Law School," appeared on the architecture page of the *New York Times* on June 7. The author, architecture editor Paul Goldberger, reported with pride there is a new law school (City University Law School) at Queens College in Flushing that has a new curriculum that is "an alternative to traditional law schools," a curriculum that "is aimed at the student who sees law as an instrument of social change rather than as a part of the world of business and finance."

Since this new law school didn't begin until 1983, and didn't graduate its first movers and shakers until 1986, one wonders how the Bill of Rights (1790); the Thirteenth (1865), Fourteenth (1866), and Fifteenth (1870) Amendments; the Sherman Antitrust Act (1890); the New Deal (1933–1945); the Fair Deal (1945–1952); the Civil Rights Voting Act (1964); and all those environmental protection acts, among thousands of other laws, were ever enacted. But the point of this essay is not to challenge the new law school's bill of fare but the architecture that houses it.

According to the *Times* article, the founders of this new school "were attempting to create a new kind of legal education and sought an architectural form that would be appropriate to it." The question for discussion here is not whether the school's interior design is, or is not, "appropriate" for such a new curriculum but something more basic: Can there ever be a building scheme that is more suited for one kind of legal education than for another? If so, a school that specialized in personal injury law would be specially built with narrow, intersecting corridors, a model of the lower Manhattan grid which produces dozens of bent-fender lawsuits daily. Students studying family law would meet in a simulated playroom; those majoring in wills and estates would hold whispered seminars in funeral parlors; and young scholars planning a career in litigation would convene weekly for sparring sessions in Stillman's Gym. Law students, shaped by their school's contours, would graduate as premolded experts.

If there were, as Mr. Goldberger suggests, a relationship between the dimensions of a building and the ideas of its inhabitants, there are many buildings that could be put to better use. For instance, there are about a dozen serious contenders for the presidency in 1988, and each should be required to move a campaign headquarters to the top floors of either the World Trade Center in New York or the Sears Tower in Chicago; no other space would be as appropriate for those seeking the nation's highest office. Atria should be reserved for popular poets, songsters, and other writers of light verse. Unprincipled politicians should be given desk space in the very best building ever built for taking many sides on every issue, the Pentagon. A Ford Foundation study matching structures to their optimum use will soon take place in the subway, that is, it will soon be under way.

While we await the results, we must focus again on the "new" law school, because soon its alumni will be edging toward Wall Street's lure. If, in response, old-fashioned courses in corporate finance are added to the catalogue, will the building, the very matrix of the "alternative" curriculum, be able to handle the new (albeit traditional) load? A study by engineers indicates that no structural changes will be needed, except perhaps in the school's facade.

June 29, 1987

VII. *American History and the Law*

The "Key to the Continent" of Yesteryear

I am not a military expert, generally speaking. I make this concession even though I have twice visited West Point, once as a sprinter with my college track team and once, many years later, as a tourist with my children. On neither occasion did I audit even one class on military strategy or participate in maneuvers. Perhaps because of this lack of formal training I have always been baffled by the military mind. These thoughts (or doubts) became more focused this summer when I visited Fort Ticonderoga.

The fort nestles on a promontory on the west bank of Lake Champlain where the lake and Wood Creek join. It would be an ideal spot for a summer camp, but instead there is a fort, with guns bristling in all directions. I recognize that forts had to be built *somewhere* in the wilderness, and I remember from all those movie Westerns that the U.S. Army dotted the frontier with them.

Forts were the places where the troops were garrisoned and the cannons were in place to protect them from the Indians. To prove the steadfastness of their mission many of them were named Fort Defiance (as was one of the forts in the Ticonderoga complex), which immediately gave the Red Man a clue to the White Man's intransigence. Had the Indians employed a psychiatrist instead of bows and arrows they would have dislodged the pale intruders early on.

What most attracted my attention at Fort Ticonderoga was the statement in the brochure that it was the "Key to the Continent," that whoever held the fort thereby held North America. That statement was not just the puffery of the ticket hawkers but was, rather, the considered opinions of Generals Montcalm, Abercromby, Amherst, Burgoyne, and maybe even of George Washington. It is hard to believe that this idyllic spot, a spot that is perfect for bird-watching, could have (or be thought to have) momentous military significance.

Military bases, it seems to me (a person who has never audited   *161* even one lecture on strategy, although I have visited West Point twice), have importance for either one of two reasons: they may have a genuine strategic location, like Thermopylae or the Straits of Gibraltar; or they may be symbolic and represent, as it were, the forward planting of the flag, like Quemoy and Matsu. For those too young to remember, the presidential campaign of 1960 was waged partly on the issue of whether Mr. Nixon or Mr. Kennedy would better defend Quemoy and Matsu, two tiny islands in the China Sea. It was argued during that campaign that whoever controlled Quemoy and Matsu would control Asia, and whoever controlled Asia would control the world.

But whether strategically critical or only symbolic, the grim fact is that more than 10,000 young soldiers—French, Indian, British, Canadian, and American—died in the defense of, or the capture of, Fort Ticonderoga. While dead is dead, I suppose a casualty is harder to accept when the military prize is symbolic, for then its importance may exist only in the minds of the High Command. The fort would seem to be such a place because Lake Champlain, for all its beauty and length, seems to go nowhere; at least one cannot get from there to the New York City line by water because the Hudson River is not navigable north of Albany. So, while controlling Fort Ticonderoga is better than not controlling it, and it is surely good for the national ego if it is your flag that flutters o'er its battlements, the "Key to the Continent" (in my inexpert opinion) it never was.

The problem is that it is not always easy to separate something genuinely strategic from something imaginary. Although it is hard to believe there is a master plan in the Kremlin for the swift capture of Fort Ticonderoga, the French and British of the 1750s viewed it differently. And while we may consider Xerxes' defeat to be the beginning of the Golden Age of Western Civilization, there were surely some Neville Chamberlain-type Greeks who argued that Leonidas ought not waste his time or troops at far-distant Thermopylae because nothing that happened there could possibly affect Athens or Sparta.

And so the military always prevails because we can never be sure whether a piece of territory is necessary for our survival or is just some general's ego trip. Rather than take a chance, we do battle every time. Is far-distant tiny Nicaragua a threat to our security? I would say no. But since I never even audited one course on military strategy, that would be privately speaking.

September 8, 1986

At Least George III Balanced the Budget

Except for the fact that it caused the American Revolution, the Stamp Act was a perfect piece of legislation. Neither Kemp-Roth nor Lord Keynes could construct a tax law more marvelous; if the act were still the law, the government could fund all of the Pentagon's outer-space fantasies and still cheerfully be able to bail out Chrysler, Packard, and Kaiser-Fraser.

> For every . . . pleading . . . in any Court of law within the British Colonies and plantations in America, a stamp duty of three pence.

Considering the amount of litigation in our land, this clause would raise billions of dollars annually. But more important than even the revenue would be the strict standard necessarily imposed on government lawyers. The new Reagan administration has already announced limitations on profligacy; and were the act still in effect, the attorney general could pleasantly agree that many new proposed government lawsuits sounded useful and ingenious. But he would be obliged to ask: "Is that pleading worth the three-cent fee?" With that as the statutory measure of legal worth, more than one federal and state agency would have to disband.

> For all dice . . . sold or used . . . the sum of ten shillings.

Were that the law today, children would not be permitted to spend every rainy afternoon playing Monopoly, imperiously trading the Orange (St. James, Tennessee, and New York) for the Dark Blue (Broadway and Park Place). One result would be that millions of people would no longer be passing Go, hence not collecting $200. Immediately, and without any interference from the Federal Reserve Board, inflation would dramatically subside. And there would be no need to continue with the Department of Justice's massive four-year investigation as to why the identical little green house should cost $50 on Connecticut Avenue but $200 on Pennsylvania Avenue.

> For every almanack or calendar for any one particular year
> . . . a stamp duty of four pence.

Absent the act we have become the most wasteful calendar-consuming country in history, as if our days and weeks and months were without limit. Too long we have boasted that our standard of living was the highest in the world because we consumed eighteen calendars per capita. No American likes to believe that people in underdeveloped countries have as many Tuesdays a year as we do. A special calendar tax would not only produce a torrent of revenue, enough to fund every senator's pet water project, but would force some calendar consolidations. For instance, barber shops might forgo their odalisque versions in favor of Airline Art, winging into Houston. And that strangest calendar of all, the government calendar that requires all presidents to be born on a Monday or Friday would, one hopes, be eliminated.

The Stamp Act produced so much revenue so effortlessly that a convention of New Dealers and academics was called to devise spending schemes. They agreed to recommend: two mail deliveries on Sundays (absorbing $1.4 billion a year); paying OPEC $75 a barrel for oil; and building a fleet of B-17 Flying Fortress bombers. The bombers would not only use up several billion unneeded dollars thanks to cost overruns, but would, it was argued, reverse the worldwide trend toward ever deadlier weapons; it was even suggested that the Soviets might respond by increasing their cavalry. Gatherings of New Dealers are often nostalgic.

The Stamp Act taxed all advertisements; taxed college degrees; and even taxed playing cards. It was almost like living in New York City in 1981, except that the colonists didn't have to pay a haircut tax or a garage tax. How come then that they revolted and we are so passive? Perhaps we ought gather a posse of aroused citizens and dump tea bags into Sheepshead Bay; even then the sales tax would probably not be reduced, because the mayor, unlike the British Empire, is no soft touch. Or we could refuse—

absolutely, irrevocably refuse—to quarter British troops in our homes. But Prime Minister Thatcher would probably not even wince in public; the British are so unflappable.

The only thing we cannot do is declare our Independence, because those who resisted the Stamp Act did that for us. Viewed from that vantage—the vantage of liberty—is it not better to pay the bizarre and excessive taxes imposed on us by our own confused government than to pay even three pence to those red-coated tyrants?

March 12, 1981

The Attorney General's Dilemma

There is an unseemly controversy between Supreme Court Justices Brennan and Stevens (on the one hand) and Attorney General Meese and perhaps Justice Rehnquist (on the other) as to the original intent of the draftsmen of the Constitution. Each side, like Fundamentalist preachers interpreting the Bible, sees every word of the Constitution as supporting its own particular judicial philosophy. This essay suggests that both sides are wrong, because the only intent the Framers had was to adjourn sine die and go home. They had just spent the hot summer (May 25–September 17, 1787) in Philadelphia, not New York or San Francisco or Saratoga or Nice. As one restless delegate from Connecticut put it: how many weekends can you spend with a box lunch looking at one cracked bell?

Both Justice Brennan (the so-called activist) and Attorney General Meese (who prides himself on his conservatism) are wrong for a fundamental reason: they are assuming, contrary to fact, that there was a basic philosophy rooted in the Constitution, some pervasive jurisprudence that would give the law a consistency through the generations and centuries. But alas, from 1787 until at least November 1985, the law has been as ad hoc as each year's pennant races, yielding, each season, to the current heavy hitters.

The drafting of the Constitution is itself a perfect example of shifting political power. The facts do not inspire reverence for the delegates' Original Intent. Shortly after Independence, the new Nation adopted the Articles of Confederation and Perpetual Union. Although now almost forgotten, that precious document was considered by those who had declared Independence to be the perfect culmination of their heroic struggle. It assured both Union (the thirteen states would be forever united as one country, with a Congress to enact all common laws) and Liberty (the states, with their charters and guarantees of free speech, free press, and free religion, would retain a measure of separate autonomy).

The theory of the day was that all strong central governments, *167* by definition, were a threat to liberty; for liberty had been lost just a few years earlier when the power had been concentrated in the British Parliament. And it must be underscored that all basic liberties—of speech, press, religion, and assembly—were absolutely secure under the Articles of Confederation in every state. So strongly did Americans believe that their freedoms were guaranteed by the separateness of the thirteen states that the Articles of Confederation, which by unanimous agreement had to be "inviolably observed by every State," could not be altered or amended except by the unanimous consent of all thirteen.

But a decade later, in 1787, there were those (the Federalists) who began to campaign for a strong central government and for a new Constitution to provide it. The anti-Federalists were in vehement opposition; as their most famous spokesman, Patrick Henry, said, "The first thing I have at heart is American *liberty*." Since the Articles of Confederation could not be altered except by the unanimous vote of all the states, the anti-Federalists were on unassailable legal ground when Rhode Island refused to send a delegation to the Constitutional Convention in Philadelphia.

As far as Rhode Island was concerned the original intent of that convention was nothing other than a coup against liberty. The Rhode Island General Assembly sent a letter to the convention's president, George Washington, which stated that its absence was "actuated by that great principle which hath ever been the characteristic of this State, the Love of true Constitutional liberty, and the fear we have of making innovations on the Rights and Liberties of the Citizens at large." The assembly reminded Mr. Washington that the Articles could not be altered, except by the unanimous vote of all thirteen states, and that it (Rhode Island) was not consenting: "You will impute it, Sir, to our being diffident of power and an apprehension of dissolving a compact, which was framed by the Wisdom of Men who gloried in being instrumental in preserving the Religious and Civil rights of a Multitude of people."

Since the Federalists could not muster the thirteen votes, one would suppose that any alteration of the Articles was legally and morally and constitutionally impossible. But then the Federalists, the sainted Framers of the Constitution, did a remarkable thing:

the Constitutional Convention simply changed the rules. Henceforth, instead of unanimity, the consents of only nine states would be required for changes. Since changing the rules in mid-stream to accommodate the personal wishes of the group in temporary power is the very definition of "activism," one wonders why the attorney general cites the "original intent" of the Framers as an argument against change. It would be almost as if a president who doubled the national debt were to campaign for a constitutional amendment requiring a balanced budget.

But Mr. Meese is faced with a more fundamental inconsistency. The original intent of the Founding Fathers, as set forth in the Articles of Confederation and Perpetual Union, was to have all law enforcement conducted by the several states. Hence the Articles provided for no Justice Department and no attorney general. Therefore, if Mr. Meese were sincere about following the Founders' original intent he would resign. I wonder if he appreciates his dilemma.

November 20, 1985

The Old Federalism

Ronald Reagan, a twentieth-century grandee, and Patrick Henry, an eighteenth-century rabblerouser, agree on one constitutional issue—power should be exercised not by a central government but by the states, by local folks. "States," said Mr. Henry in opposing the adoption of the Constitution, "are the soul of a confederation." In his new, classic study of the Anti-Federalists of the 1780s (*What The Antifederalists Were For*, University of Chicago Press, 1981), the late Professor Herbert J. Storing summed up the position of Patrick Henry, Edmund Randolph, Elbridge Gerry, George Mason, and Luther Martin, great patriots all, as follows: "It was thought to have been demonstrated, historically and theoretically, that free, republican governments could extend only over a relatively small territory with a homogeneous population."

In New York City, that would mean that block associations should be sovereign. In that spirit, let us consider the following look to the future.

The West 181st Street Block Association (Manhattan) voted to condemn the Argentine take-over of the Falkland Islands. To implement that condemnation, the association's Foreign Office froze all Argentine assets in local banks, a move that would have only limited immediate impact because there were neither Argentine assets nor local banks on 181st Street (Manhattan). The association also voted to recall Marvin the Deli-Man, its ambassador to Buenos Aires. But the full force of the fateful decision was blunted when it was discovered that Marvin had not yet taken up his Southern Hemisphere duties; his wife, Shirley, said he couldn't go to the Argentine capital until he fixed the kitchen faucet. And so Marvin's credentials have been kept in his diplomatic pouch and stored in the freezer; they have not yet been presented to Nicanor Costa Mendez, Argentina's foreign minister.

Up north, the Dyckman Street Block Association, representing a strong Irish constituency, took the opposite view and condemned the British attack on Port Stanley. Secretary of State

Haig, representing the central government, was fearful of a split in American ranks. He extended his shuttle diplomacy to Manhattan and raced to an emergency meeting of the Dyckman Street cabinet with a plea for unity, only to learn that the only subject discussed was alternate street parking. To the secretary's credit, he maintained his cherublike smile.

A Bronx government, located on the Grand Concourse, asked the Pentagon for two nuclear-powered submarines. A braided admiral denied the request because that particular nation was landlocked. But he was overruled on the ground that since the Grand Concourse nation also had neither engineers nor sailors to operate the sophisticated vessel, the lack of a coast was irrelevant. In return, Grand Concourse voted to condemn Cuba in the United Nations.

While foreign affairs dominated much of the metropolitan scene, pocketbook issues were more important inland. In Hershey, Pennsylvania, for example, the Parliament voted to ban the importation of all foreign chocolate on the ground that a strong domestic cocoa industry was essential for national security. The Swiss were, predictably, upset, and Secretary Haig had to add Hershey to his shuttle itinerary of London, Buenos Aires, Cairo, Tel Aviv, and Dyckman Street. This time, however, diplomacy was successful. Hershey rescinded its ban on chocolate imports (thus saving free trade) and, in exchange, the central government in Washington agreed that it would, as part of its strategic reserves, stockpile Mr. Goodbars.

This Balkanization of America led to a problem in elementary schools from coast to coast. Once upon a time, third- and fourth-graders prided themselves on their ability to recite the names of all the state capitals—Tallahassee, Montpelier, Albany, Sacramento, Trenton, Lansing. But now even computers couldn't keep up. For instance, the 181st Street Block Association established its government in the Kentucky Fried Chicken Building, on the north side of 181st Street, just east of Broadway. Ten thousand, or 20,000, other American nations were similarly established. Only the flag makers, the national anthem composers, and the cartographers prospered. And, of course, the American position at the United Nations was greatly strengthened; one vote to condemn Israel (for having celebrated Passover) lost 20,759 to 124 (with France abstaining).

Despite that advantage, some Constitutionalists were uneasy about the return to the days of the Articles of Confederation. To reverse the trend, two East Side block associations (74th and Fifth Avenue and 73d and Fifth Avenue) actually merged. That new union was, its leaders proclaimed, a harbinger of a greater national union to come. One local East 74th Street politician likened the merger to the Congress of Vienna of 1815; another to the international conference at Dumbarton Oaks. Folks who live on Fifth and 74th Street aren't modest. But some of their self-proclaimed grandiose idealism was discounted when it was reported that the first act passed by the new joint legislature was a reduction in the capital gains rate.

When each American nation started printing its own money and its own stamps and designing its own subway tokens (with all those portraits of local politicians), most people began to conclude that Patrick Henry had been wrong and that Daniel Webster and Abraham Lincoln had been right, that the Union *had* to be preserved. There may be faults with a strong central government, but for two centuries a united America has been the freest and noblest and most prosperous country in history. And so, throughout the land, the new principalities disbanded.

As they took down the newly designed flag from atop the Kentucky Fried Chicken Building on 181st Street, just east of Broadway, for the very last time, Ambassador Marvin the Deli-Man said it best: "I even have plans for my unused striped pants and morning coat. I'm going to save them for my daughter Amy's wedding. She's only a little girl now, but maybe she'll marry one of those princes from Fifth Avenue and 73d Street. Those things happen, but only in America."

May 17, 1982

The Commerce Clause and Abraham Lincoln

James Madison died in 1836 so it is probably too late to challenge his last will and testament. But that document contains one legacy, one precedent, that troubles our nation to this day: Madison apparently assumed that he personally owned the biggest news that he ever made, that is, the drafting of the Constitution. And so he bequeathed the expected income from the publication of his *Notes of Debates in the Federal Convention of 1787* to his wife, Dolley. The will even included an unabashed sales pitch for the *Notes*, asserting that they will be "particularly gratifying to the people of the United States, and to all who take an interest in the progress of political science and the cause of true liberty." It was Madison's hope that the monetary value of the *Notes* would increase with time, and that was one reason why he did not permit their publication until after his death.

The point here is that the *Notes*, the only definitive contemporaneous writing on the drafting of the Constitution (Charles Evans Hughes said that the *Notes* were "the most direct approach to the intention of the makers of the Constitution") should not have belonged to James Madison; they should have belonged to the American people. Nobody forced Madison to be the scribe, but having volunteered he ought not have been in business for himself. Nobody (as far as I know) has ever criticized Mr. Madison for his unseemly last will, which may prove that Teflon is older than we think.

What prompts this essay is the Supreme Court's recent decision in *Harper & Row v. Nation Enterprises,* which held that President Ford personally owned the biggest news of his administration, that is, how former President Nixon was pardoned. Mr. Ford, in his autobiography, *A Time to Heal,* discussed the circumstances of the pardon. His publisher, Harper and Row, had sold to *Time* magazine (for $12,500) the exclusive right to print prepublication excerpts, and *Time* chose to run the story on the pardon. *The Nation* magazine received an unauthorized copy of the Ford manuscript, and itself published the story of the pardon, using some (300 out of 2,250) of Mr. Ford's own words. *Time* felt pre-empted, and canceled. Whereupon Harper and Row sued, claiming that *The Nation* had violated its copyright. The Supreme Court upheld Harper and Row's claim on the ground that *The Nation* had quoted some of Mr. Ford's own words, for under the copyright law particular language or expression can be protected; but not, of course, the news itself.

Mr. Ford is not a poet, not an essayist, and not a phrase-turner. His version of the pardon was important not because of his prose style or felicitous language but only because of that which was suggested: that perhaps a deal had been cut whereby Vice President Ford had succeeded to the presidency in exchange for promising to pardon Mr. Nixon. That might not be news to the cynic, but it would be quite an admission from Mr. Ford. President Ford is free to explain the Nixon pardon, or be silent. But he ought not be able to *sell* us that news, any more than James Madison ought to have been able to sell the *Notes*.

President Lincoln arrived at Gettysburg on November 19, 1863, after a wearisome train ride from Washington. When Edward Everett, the principal orator, had finally finished, the president, in his familiar stovepipe hat and black frock, rose to speak:

> On my way to this solemn occasion to dedicate this sacred ground to our honored dead, I jotted down some notes on the back of an envelope. It is a dandy talk, friends, one of my best, full of unique and quotable expressions that, I predict, will be recited by schoolchildren long after we are gone and forgotten. I've sent my notes, by special courier, to my publisher in New York, who hopes to have a printed version in your bookstore by the first week in December. The hardcover version will retail for $3.75 if purchased before Christmas, and $4.25 thereafter. I urge you, my friends, on this solemn occasion, to avoid disappointment. A deposit of only 50 cents will secure your copy. I should note, too, that the TV rights, movie rights, serial rights, and foreign rights, except for Canada, have not yet been negotiated, and those interested are urged to contact my publisher at once.

July 18, 1985

Judge Bork and the Foreign Trade Deficit

The only unifying result that emerged from the Bork confirmation hearings was the solution to the nation's $180 billion a year foreign trade deficit. That surprising economic breakthrough came, unexpectedly, amid some unlikely banter among the senators on the Judiciary Committee and the nominee; the discussion concerned whether Judge Bork would, or would not, follow precedents.

The judge gave assurances that if elevated to the Supreme Court he would not upset old decisions, even if he disagreed with them intellectually, if they had become woven into the nation's "fabric." At that point the senators and judge agreed, amid gentle laughter, that the Legal Tender cases—the cases that ultimately upheld the government's right to print paper money that was valid as legal tender—would be just such an example. And there was the insight, the flash: the Legal Tender cases, ignored for over a century, provide the solution that might yet save our country from its deluge of Toyota-caused debt.

The historical facts are these: The Congress, in order to finance the Civil War, passed the Legal Tender Act of 1862. That act authorized the Treasury not only to issue paper money (the so-called greenbacks), but to make that money legal tender for all debts, private and public. A total of $450 million of such folding currency was printed and circulated, which bought a lot of muskets and blue uniforms. But since that new printing-press money could not be converted into real money (that is, gold or silver specie), it sold at a large discount. A certain Mrs. Hepburn from Kentucky once signed a note promising to pay one Henry Griswold 11,250 "dollars," which she did. But she paid in the new depreciated medium. Mr. Griswold sued, arguing that "dollars" meant the genuine article, like the kind that he had loaned to Mrs. Hepburn, not the inky newsprint stuff.

This first challenge to the Legal Tender Act, *Hepburn v. Griswold*, reached the Supreme Court in 1870. Chief Justice Salmon P. Chase, writing for the majority, found the act to be unconstitutional. His arguments read as if they are part of the current debate on constitutional exegesis. The chief justice first looked to Article I, which enumerates all the powers granted to Congress, and found that the power to print paper legal tender was not among them: "All legislative power granted by the Constitution belongs to Congress; but it has no legislative power which is not granted."

Indeed, that strict construction point was reinforced because the Constitution does authorize the Congress, specifically, "to coin Money." That meant, reasoned the Court, that the Constitutional Convention, in dealing with the nation's currency, meant to give Congress the power of coinage but not of printing.

The majority opinion then explored further the issue of original intent. It noted that the Northwest Ordinance was adopted by the Congress of the Confederation in the same year (1787) as the Constitutional Convention's deliberations; hence the ordinance was analyzed to see if it would provide a clue as to the Constitution's original and true intent. A clue was discerned from the ordinance's provision that "no law ought ever to be made, or have force in the same territory, that shall in any manner whatever interfere with or affect private contracts."

The Court reasoned that since the newfangled money interfered with private contracts it would not have been allowed as legal tender in the territories beyond the Ohio River; hence, it was concluded, such wampum could not be allowed in the Union itself.

Thus, *Hepburn v. Griswold*, in a frenzy of strict construction, held that paper money could not be legal tender in the United States. But despite the force of its logic, *Hepburn* was soon overruled (see *Juilliard v. Greenman*, 1884); and greenbacks flourished again. But if *Hepburn* could be overruled it could also be reinstated, for in the law nothing is ever decided finally until it is decided right. And with the reinstatement of *Hepburn*, paper money would again be passé; and so would our nation's trade deficit, for how would Japanese companies transport all that gold and silver specie back home? A fleet of cargo planes powerful enough to fly a battalion of tanks to trouble spots across the seas could not lift all the coins that would be spent each week in the

United States for all those Toyotas, Mazdas, Nissans, Hondas, and Mitsubishis, not to speak of cameras and sushi. Specially fitted tankers, with steel-reinforced holds, would have to be designed; and hundreds, then thousands, of warehouses would have to be built as those tankers relentlessly discharged their clanging cargo. In a few months Honshu Island would sink under the weight, and Japan's bold attempt to dominate the economies of the world would be submerged forever.

It is not the purpose of this essay to take sides, one way or the other, on the Bork nomination. But if you want to overrule the later Legal Tender cases and thereby restore America's trade surplus, Judge Bork would seem to be a more promising candidate than most.

October 23, 1987

Post-Postmortem

Although the preacher (said to be Solomon) cautioned long ago that "there is nothing new under the sun" (Ecclesiastes 1:9), a recent book on the Sacco-Vanzetti case (*Postmortem*, by William Young and David E. Kaiser, University of Massachusetts Press) has set a new world record for staleness. Almost everything contained in this "new" book, published in 1985, was said, and said much better, in 1927. See *The Case of Sacco and Vanzetti*, written by Felix Frankfurter, then a professor at the Harvard Law School (published by Little, Brown). But the thrust of this essay is to suggest that its sixty-year tardiness is not *Postmortem*'s principal failing; its real fault is that, in its rush to print, *Postmortem* has missed the point.

The basic Sacco-Vanzetti facts were these: A paymaster and his guard were robbed and murdered at 3 P.M. on April 15, 1920, in South Braintree, Massachusetts. Some weeks later, two radical immigrants, Sacco (a shoemaker) and Vanzetti (a fish peddler), were arrested and charged with the crime. Their arrest was during a time of national hysteria, symbolized by the Palmer Raids (named for A. Mitchell Palmer, the attorney general of the United States, who had ordered the rounding up and deportation of all foreign Reds). Sacco and Vanzetti assumed at first that their arrest was part of that national antiradical campaign.

The murder trial began May 31, 1921; the defendants were found guilty seven weeks later. A summary of the trial, as described by both books, follows:

1. The witnesses who testified that they had seen Sacco and Vanzetti commit the crime were, each and every one of them, incredible. For instance, one witness (Mary E. Splaine), who had been unable to identify Sacco immediately after the crime, swore on the stand that he was the culprit because she recalled seeing that he had a "good-sized hand" and that his hair was between two and two and one-half inches long (such observations having been made while the gangsters were making their blazing geta-

way in a fast-moving car, and she was at least sixty feet away). See Frankfurter, pp. 12–14; *Postmortem*, pp. 46–63.

2. The alibi evidence was conclusive that both Sacco and Vanzetti were elsewhere at the time of the crime. Sacco was proven to have been at the Italian consulate in Boston, arranging for a passport; and thirteen separate, unbiased witnesses testified that Vanzetti was at his regular stand in Plymouth, selling fish. See Frankfurter, p. 10 and p. 30; *Postmortem*, pp. 79–84.

3. The evidence (including a confession) was overwhelming, if not conclusive, that the murders had been committed by the Morelli Gang of Providence, which had specialized in that very kind of crime for years. Frankfurter, p. 68 and pp. 92–100; *Postmortem*, pp. 134–157.

4. The only "hard" evidence supporting the guilt of Sacco and Vanzetti was the testimony of Captain Proctor, head of the Massachusetts State Police, who was something of a ballistics expert:

Q: Have you an opinion as to whether bullet No. 3 was fired from the Colt automatic [Sacco's pistol]?
A: I have.
Q: And what is your opinion?
A: My opinion is that it is consistent with being fired from that pistol.

On the basis of that one statement, the trial judge charged the jury that "it was [Sacco's] pistol that fired the bullet that caused the death" of the guard.

But after the trial, Captain Proctor explained in an affidavit that his testimony had been a trick, a deceitful play on words. He explained that he had repeatedly advised the district attorney that he could *not* say that Sacco's gun had fired the fatal bullet, whereupon artful language was devised that was technically accurate (the bullet was "consistent" with having been fired from Sacco's gun because it was "consistent" with having been fired from *any* Colt automatic, of which there were tens or hundreds of thousands). Captain Proctor's recanting affidavit was submitted in support of a motion for a new trial, a motion which Judge Webter Thayer denied. See Frankfurter, pp. 76–82; *Postmortem*, pp. 92–94.

Postmortem does go beyond the Frankfurter book to establish one new (probable) fact: even assuming that bullet No. 3 had been fired from Sacco's weapon, it was probably fired by the prosecution itself for use in the trial, and switched to make it appear as if it had come from the body of the murdered guard. But that fraud (if *Postmortem* is correct), however gross, was not decisive because evidence was not what mattered. Note that there was no attempt to link either Sacco or Vanzetti to any of the other three bullets extracted from the victims, yet some gunman had put them there. And recall that Sacco himself was proven to have been at the office of the Italian consulate in Boston at the time of the crime, yet he was convicted.

But why didn't the evidence matter? That is the basic inquiry of Professor Frankfurter's book; and that is the very point missed by *Postmortem*. Frankfurter concluded that the key to the trial was not evidence but prejudice:

> Outside the courtroom the Red hysteria was rampant; it was allowed to dominate within. The prosecutor systematically played on the feelings of the jury by exploiting the unpatriotic and despised beliefs of Sacco and Vanzetti, and the judge allowed him thus to divert and pervert the jury's mind. [P. 46]

> By systematic exploitation of the defendants' alien blood, their imperfect knowledge of English, their unpopular social views, and their opposition to the war, the District Attorney invoked against them a riot of political passion and patriotic sentiment; and the trial judge connived at—one had almost written, cooperated in—the process. [P. 59]

Thus, when Vanzetti was on the stand, the D.A. made these inquiries, which the court allowed:

Q: So you left Plymouth, Mr. Vanzetti, in May, 1917, to dodge the draft, did you?
A: Yes, sir.

Q: When this country was at war, you ran away, so you would not have to fight as a soldier?

A: Yes.

In case the jury missed the point, the routine was repeated with Sacco:

Q: And in order to show your love for this United States of America when she was about to call upon you to become a soldier you ran away to Mexico. . . . Did you go to Mexico to avoid being a soldier for this country that you loved?

A: Yes. [Frankfurter, pp. 47–48]

As the trial ended and these radical, foreign, antiwar draft dodgers stood accused of murder, Judge Thayer began his charge to the jury. It was more like the charge up San Juan Hill: "Although you knew that such [jury] service would be arduous, painful and tiresome, yet you, like the true soldier, responded to that call in the spirit of supreme American loyalty. There is no better word in the English language than 'loyalty'!" (Frankfurter, p. 64).

But the authors of *Postmortem* seem to believe that Sacco and Vanzetti died natural deaths, for this is how they have evaluated Judge Thayer's behavior: "for the most part he carefully kept any prejudice out of the trial record, exhorting the jury to judge the defendants as if their forefathers had sailed on the *Mayflower*" (p. 10).

The preacher (said to be Solomon) cautioned long ago that we could not rely on man's shifting version of the truth because "of making many books there is no end" (Ecclesiastes 12:12).

March 5, 1986

VIII. *The Law Distorted*

Reductio ad Absurdum

The world record for reduction, until 1980, was the black hole; stars, some of them hundreds of times larger than our sun, have constricted to the size of a tennis ball. The black hole is so compact, hence its gravitational pull is so strong, that not even light can escape. Therefore, the presence of black holes is confirmed every time you scan the heavens and don't see any. Scientists and lawyers think alike.

In 1980, the long reign of black holes ended, and a new record for compactness was set when Oxford University Press published its *Oxford Companion to the Law*. To quote from the book's jacket blurb: "Spanning the full history of Western law, from the dawn of Greek and Roman civilization to the present, the entries cover legal history and philosophy, comparative law, international law, and the main legal systems that share the common Western legal tradition."

It's all done in just 1,366 pages, including appendices. The Harvard Law Library does the same job, but in 1,300,000 volumes.

The Oxford University Press has proved what laymen have always known, but what lawyers never admit—that the law is overblown. With the *Companion to the Law* as a standard for compression, the bloat should be squeezed out of all parts of the law. If comparable condensations were made, the IBM trial, now in its eleventh year and five billionth document, would take, in its entirety, only a half-hour of Judge Edelstein's time. Law school, instead of three years, would be completed on any rainy afternoon. Everyone could go to Harvard or Yale, although there would be some disruptions because there would be a twenty-fifth law school reunion every morning and every afternoon. Judges might be relieved, because no brief would exceed one sentence; there would probably be a lot of semicolons in antitrust cases. The Justice Department would be manned by one part-time paralegal (who, nonetheless, would require Senate confirmation). And the FTC, SEC, CAB, FCC, and OPA (for old times' sake) would share one office, located in the basement of the abandoned Department of Energy Building.

There would be no lawyers, save for some oldsters who still owned Blackstone's *Commentaries*, because there would be no more litigation; litigation would stop because statutes of limitations would be three minutes for contracts, five minutes for torts, and never long enough to enable anyone to begin a lawsuit.

While there were great celebrations throughout the land because there were no more lawyers and no more lawsuits, a hitch developed: if the shriveling were applied to criminal law, an armed robber might be sentenced to ten minutes at hard labor; if portal-to-portal time were applied (remember John L. Lewis), the desperadoes might not be given enough time even to change clothes. But the law solved that problem with a formula it uses best—the exception. For instance, the draft is for all persons between nineteen and twenty-one, except women; abortions are allowed for all women, except poor ones. Therefore, the *Oxford Companion* pucker would be applied to all persons except criminals. Although the civil liberties people will launch one of those never-ending challenges to the constitutionality of that exception, fortunately the whole matter will be disposed of in under two minutes.

Although the *Oxford Companion* reduces the entire body of Western law to one microfiche, it was soon discovered that even it had plenty of water that could be squeezed out. The discussion of law in the United States, particularly, includes many extraneous passages: "The U.S. has contributed disappointing little to the literature of legal history or jurisprudence" and "Prior to 1850, educational requirements for admission to the Bar were frequently lax and, on occasion, nonexistent. Since then standards have been steadily rising" (p. 1,264).

Comments on English institutions are not all that favorable, either: "Since 1945 and particularly since 1965 there has been a very widespread fall in the qualities of M.P.'s and in public regard for Parliament" (p. 929).

And some individuals, who one might think would be honored by being included in so compact a book, are soundly criticized. William Teulon Swan Stallybrass, who taught law at Oxford, is described as "not a great lecturer"; Henry Powle, who was appointed Master of the Rolls in 1690, "left no mark as a judge"; and Sir Richard Rainsford, "a respected but mediocre lawyer . . . left no mark in the law." Indeed, if the names of undistinguished law professors and judges are to be included, many readers of this *Law Journal* could fill up 1,366 pages off the tops of their heads. On the other hand, some rather important persons in the law, such as Justices Hugo Black and Robert Jackson, have been omitted.

Tart comments are not meant only for the otherwise anonymous, for the work of Jean Jacques Rousseau is described as "incomplete and logically defective," and our own hallowed John Marshall is criticized for his five-volume work, *The Life of George Washington,* which the *Companion* depicts as "hastily written and disappointing." James Wilson, who was a central figure at our Constitutional Convention, is described as "greedy and ambitious"; the fact that he signed the Declaration of Independence is omitted. I would guess that the *Companion to the Law* could be edited from 1,366 pages to about 450. If that were so, and were all other aspects of the law reduced *pro tanto,* law school would then take only forty-five minutes, and that one part-time paralegal running the Justice Department might have to be discharged.

But on reflection, the *Oxford Companion* may miss the point. Cataloguing names and snippets of decisions, albeit alphabetically, reveals no more about the essence of the law than a telephone book reveals about the spirit of a city. The essence of the law is one thing and one thing only—ideas. And ideas can't be squashed or confined to some tightly bound compendium. Some ideas that take only a few words to state—freedom of speech, due process—are the opposite of black holes, because each one of them can light up the world. They've much to learn about the law at Oxford University.

July 31, 1980

Of Tennessee and Dinosaurs

The law, which has been unable to decide such froufrou as whether the national speed limit ought to be 55 m.p.h. or 75, or whether people who were but good friends are entitled to alimony, has undertaken to decide how and when the universe was created. And quite properly so, for the theory of evolution, the current wisdom about creation, is contrary to the spirit of our legal system. When Tennessee enacted a law in the 1920s to protect its children from learning Darwinism, memorialized in the overwrought drama, *Inherit the Wind*, Tennessee knew well what it was doing. The pity has been that the other states, or the League of Nations, didn't pass a similar statute. But now, finally, there is hope, for the new 97th Congress will probably give such a bill quick passage, along with a law to outlaw inflation.

Evolution is a dangerous concept for several reasons. For one, it is just too dawdling; it takes millions or billions of years to solve every problem. From some slithering cell at the water's edge—I think it must have been at the beach at Coney Island—it took eons for there to be monkeys, then apes, and finally, Man, roller-coasting through history. While the law itself is not a particularly speedy process, it could not abide *such* delays. That is, a billion years is too long even for those who are drafting the tax reform bill.

But if the means of evolution (change imperceptible) are unacceptable to the legal system, the ends of evolution are worse. As explained by Darwin, in the long history of animals and plants only the strong have survived. Never has evolution taken one halting step backward to accommodate some tree that could not quite reach the sunlight. But the purpose of the law is the opposite; it is to protect the sparrows and snail darters of the world. If evolution's principle were imported into our legal system, oil companies (for instance) would be given depletion allowances, and giant automobile companies (for instance) would be given government loans, and only poor people (for instance) would serve in the army.

Beyond its crawling pace and might-is-right ends, there is a third aspect of evolution that must have motivated Tennessee's legislature. Evolution is just plain boring. Why should the boys and girls of Nashville be kept indoors on a nice spring day to learn about the million-year history of the beetle (Coleoptera) and the fern (Filicineae). The law, which focuses on such excitement as the drafting of wills and the transfer of real property, abhors dullness.

Although the law has been fighting evolution—and wisely so— it has, nevertheless, aped some of evolution's worst techniques. In every great law firm there are squads of associates digging for the dinosaurs of the law, called precedents. The older and more decayed the precedent, the stronger its influence. As an example, there is the history of capital punishment. In *Gregg v. Georgia*, the Supreme Court upheld capital punishment (in 1977) because capital punishment was legal when the Constitution was adopted (in 1787). And capital punishment was legal in the Colonies because of the biblical equation, "an eye for an eye." A recent archaeological-jurisprudential study indicates that it all probably started a few thousand years before the Bible, when some lawmakers in Babylon or Assyria or ancient Egypt were negotiating the passage of some reciprocal pork-barrel legislation—a dam on the Nile here in exchange for a dam on the Euphrates there—and it was agreed that when the votes were cast there would be an aye for an aye. Many of our most hallowed legal precedents are based on the equivalent of the Piltdown Man.

Clarence Darrow (Drummond in the play) is the hero of *Inherit the Wind*; and William Jennings Bryan (Brady) is the buffoon. Darrow, thumbing his red suspenders, put Bryan on the witness stand and cross-examined him about whether Jonah lived in the whale, and whether Joshua stopped the sun. Darrow's point was that since neither of those events ever happened, therefore the Bible's story of the creation must also be false. Quite a non sequitur. But beyond the fallible logic, Darrow missed the point, the heart of the matter. For the fact is that it is still too early to know whether or not those biblical accounts are true, for both depend on how Man acts today. The Book of Jonah *teaches* that Man cannot escape from his responsibility to purify the Ninevehs of this world. The Book of Joshua *teaches* that Man, if he could but gather his creative energy and spiritual fervor, could do anything, even make miracles, even stay the sun. In evolution's scheme, the sun can't stand still because nothing can vary the predetermined tempo of "progress."

The grand purpose of the law is not to set speed limits or regulate our private lives but to bring justice and mercy to Nineveh. And when the need is great and the time is short, the law's solution is sometimes miraculous. Magna Carta and our Constitution are examples of such miracles; the establishment of the Department of Energy is not. Although they were not members of the bar and probably didn't even have an LL.B. from Yale, Jonah and Joshua knew more about the law than Clarence Darrow.

December 16, 1980

In Plain English, a Bad Amendment

If an amendment proposed by Senator Hayakawa (Senate Joint Resolution 72) is adopted, onion soup gratiné will be unconstitutional. The proposal, which would prohibit all things not in the English language, has broad, non-parmesan support:

ARTICLE

Section 1. The English language shall be the official language of the United States.

Section 2. Neither the United States nor any State shall make or enforce any law which requires the use of any language other than English.

Section 3. This article shall apply to laws, ordinances, regulations, orders, programs, and policies.

Glossed over in the debates was the instant nullification of two ancient and honorable, albeit foreign language, liberties guaranteed by Article I, section 9, of the Constitution: the provisions that (1) bar *ex post facto* laws, and (2) guarantee that the writ of *habeas corpus* shall not be suspended. And so ipso facto, ipse dixit, helter-skelter, rights that originated in the Magna Carta (which, henceforth, would be referred to in its Anglicized form as The Very Very Important Document) would disappear. Disappearing, too, might be the laws of the Old Testament, such as the Ten Commandments (Hebrew), the New Testament (Greek), and the Koran (Arabic). Among the surviving statutes would be the Internal Revenue Code and the New York City Parking Regulations.

Orchestras would no longer play the Hungarian Dances, and French horn players would have to take piccolo lessons. Children could no longer play Chinese checkers, and their parents could no longer play Russian roulette. Californians would be a little colder, and museums a little smaller, for gone would be the Japanese current and Greek past.

Lawyers were rather blasé (a condition that was a misdemeanor; three blasés in a year and you could lose your driver's 191 license) about the effects of the new amendment until one judge, eager to clear his calendar for the golf season, ruled that all torts—a word that was Old French—were unconstitutional. People were able to libel each other and dent each other's fenders without fear of being sued. Some folks, especially those with faulty brakes, thought that Senate Resolution 72 was just fine. But a lot of checkers and pinochle games were being played at the bar association to while away the hours when the good news sounded: a judge somewhere had declared the defense of *res judicata* to be illegal, so that the few cases that remained could be litigated and relitigated hundreds of times. (Note for laymen: *res judicata* is the legal term that means once a case has been finally decided it is over and cannot be tried again.)

The Hayakawa Amendment would change the nature of legal discourse. Good-faith efforts, no matter how sincere, could no longer be *bona fide;* nothing could be so small as to be *de minimus;* and although meetings would go on forever because none could be adjourned *sine die,* no business could be transacted because there could never be a *quorum, et cetera, et cetera.* Citizens could adjust to those changes, except that substitute teachers wanted their *per diem* whether constitutional or not.

Suddenly our great federal system began to unravel because E Pluribus Unum was banned; whereupon scholars took a harder look at the new amendment. They determined that the amendment, properly interpreted, meant that laws had to be in very proper English, the King's English, although some doubted that Senator Hayakawa was a direct descendant of either the Tudors or the Stuarts. In parsing the proposed new law, it was discovered that its preface contained that most egregious of all grammatical errors, a split infinitive: "The Carter administration attempted to substantially broaden this mandate by proposing requirements for schools to teach other academic subjects entirely in students' native language" (127 Congressional Record, No. 61, April 27, 1981).

To the purists who had once supported the amendment, that revelation was a shocker. When another brooding professor noted that the very amendment requiring English used Arabic numbers, there was widespread feeling that the amendment was too self-contradictory for passage. Stubborn supporters of the amendment were willing to make some changes to satisfy the critics, but negotiations broke down because all *quid pro quo*s were punishable by fine.

But the greatest harm resulting from the amendment would be the abrogation of the phrase *ad coelum ad inferos*. It meant, in olden common-law days, that if you owned a piece of land, even a quarter-acre in the outskirts of Buffalo, you thereby also owned everything above the land to the sky (*ad coelum*) and everything below to the core of the earth (*ad inferos*). Even the humblest man on the smallest plot owned as high as a king. It meant you weren't just a landowner but a universe owner. Your link to the past wasn't just in the technical conveyance of some real estate that had been in the family for several generations; rather you were part of a history that went back billions of years.

In trying to make our laws parochial by focusing on the narrowest here and now, the senator is not just meddling with onion soup. He is also tampering with the Law's ancient and mystical links to the Heavens above.

June 12, 1981

The Government and Sex

This is to note, with sadness, the fifty-year decline of our government's interest in culture. Today, the government seems to be dominated by unschooled postal clerks; they have banned from the mails a pamphlet, in dull prose, about venereal disease and family planning. But in the good ol' days of 1933 the government was peopled by learned, sophisticated Harvard types; they banned James Joyce's masterpiece, *Ulysses*. Although both bans were ultimately reversed by the courts—the opinions will be discussed very briefly later—the censors' actions have left their mark.

In the years before the centerfold many youths were lured by the fact of the ban into reading *Ulysses*, in the hope of finding the good stuff. The search took days and weeks of diligence ("Mordecai, are you reading that huge book for homework?" "No, Mom, it's for extra credit"), by which time all ardor had cooled. And, finally, having found it, the reader could still not be sure. Was the United States of America really complaining about the scene where Bloom sees Gerty MacDowell on the beach (chapter 13) and each has private amatory thoughts? "Mr. Bloom watched her . . . Hot little devil all the same. Wouldn't mind."

Could it be that these government attorneys were neuters who had never had an amatory thought themselves? And could any government, even one so powerful that it ruled from ocean to ocean, actually ban thoughts? Rather than banning the books that contained these improper yearnings—thousands of new titles are published every year, and each would have to be read, catalogued, and understood—it would be administratively easier just to outlaw the naughty thoughts themselves. So the Justice Department drafted legislation that would make all amatory thoughts illegal without regard to race, religion, or the thinker's national origin.

The department was particularly proud of the law's non-discriminatory features, for which it received a letter of commen-
194 dation from B'nai B'rith. There were, of course, the usual at-

tempts to water down a simple, straightforward law. One junior draftsman suggested limiting the ban to the hours of 10 P.M. to 6 A.M., when enforcement would be the most cost-effective; he noted, in addition, that those hours were consistent with most parking regulations, so that the signs were already posted. Another practical suggestion, anticipating the oil crisis, was to limit the ban to males on even days and to females on odd days.

One congressman from Florida, with a large constituency of retirees, supported the bill but sought an exception for all persons over sixty-five and their representatives. The Teachers' Lobby supported the bill, of course ("More time for reading"), but sought an exemption for faculty on the ground of academic freedom. The bar association supported the bill but sought an exception for lawyers on the ground of the attorney-client privilege. The Authors' League supported the bill but sought an exemption for writers based on the First Amendment. Labor leaders supported the legislation because it would prevent the importation of cheap foreign thoughts, although several AFL-CIO officials wanted assurance that thoughts of unions would not, by themselves, be punishable under the new act.

I had quite forgotten about the banning of *Ulysses*, although I was one of those who, in my teens, scurried through the book in search of the illegal and the profane, until I read the recent Supreme Court decision, *Bolger v. Youngs Drug Products*. It seems that the government is still monitoring our private reading and innermost thoughts. This time Congress *really* passed a law that is as strange as the whimsical law described above. Title 39 USC Section 3001(e)(2) actually prohibits the mailing of unsolicited literature that describes contraception. As one Supreme Court justice said in the course of holding that law to be unconstitutional, it was a strange ban because it permitted the mailing of unsolicited material that facilitated or described conception "no matter how coarse or grotesque." Therefore, Section 3001(e)(2) would permit, for instance, the mailing of even the raunchiest parts of *Ulysses* but not information about how prophylactics might prevent venereal disease. One wonders what is so wonderful about VD that the government should foster it. At any rate, both Section 3001(e)(2) and the ban on *Ulysses* were declared to be unconstitutional. Even so, we suggest that the judiciary does not deal with matters of sex, or of literature, with any more distinction than the other branches of government. For instance, the key sentence in *United States v. One Book Called Ulysses* deals with that great classic on an upset stomach basis: "But my considered opinion, after long reflection, is that whilst in many places the effect of *Ulysses* on the reader undoubtedly is somewhat emetic, nowhere does it tend to be aphrodisiac."

These two bans on our reading and thinking demonstrate how far, far beyond the scope of the law is each man's private life. One explanation for the bans is that most government officials are in their fifties or sixties or seventies and are jealous of the prerogatives of youth. It's like that old cartoon which shows two ancient members of the Union League Club reading a newspaper, and one says to the other, "This Means War."

All governments, even our own, sometimes try to enforce the unenforceable by decreeing No to love and life. To which our defiant response should be the concluding phrase of *Ulysses:* "and his heart was going like mad and yes I said yes I will. Yes."

July 11, 1983

The City Council and the Great Sanhedrin

In the summer of 1985, when New York City's reservoirs were running dry and when extract of cocaine had replaced chocolate as the city's favorite sauce, the City Council was called into an emergency session. By a unanimous vote, it amended the law which designated on which Manhattan sidewalks ice-cream pops (and tofutti and Italian ices) could, and could not, be sold. And in the parliaments, knessets, legislatures, congresses, dumas, senates, assemblies, and chambers of deputies throughout the Western world, elected representatives are spending most of their working hours similarly engaged, tinkering, always tinkering, in response to this pressure group and that, with some of the world's least consequential statutes.

One solution that would free our worthy representatives from these endless annual debates is to let all interest groups have their full, unrestricted say once and for all; but after having heard every view, legislatures would enact these minor rules so that they are fixed and permanent and not subject to amendment ever again.

That is exactly how the Great Sanhedrin, which convened exactly twenty billion years ago this month, enacted the Laws of Nature. After allowing almost an endless discussion—a million-year limit on debate was agreed to for each item—the lawmakers agreed never to go through such dreary proceedings again. Hence they stipulated, unanimously, that all parties would abide forever with the final result, for better or worse.

The OPEC nations wanted to fix the boiling point of water at 5,000 degrees Fahrenheit, so that their products would always be in demand, even should automobiles become ever more efficient and even should nuclear power plants someday be properly designed. In opposition, the Third World nations argued that water should boil at 33 degrees Fahrenheit, so that tea could be made very quickly. The resulting number of 212 degrees Fahrenheit obviously represents hundreds of thousands of years of negotiation and compromise. And good to their word, OPEC members have not sought a change, although the development of the diesel engine was certainly a provocation. Although the issue is foreclosed, commentators do suggest that the Great Sanhedrin solution may have had unforeseen catastrophic results: they attribute history's thousands of wars to the world's low boiling point.

The most successful lobbying effort, as usual, was waged by the telecommunications industry. Trolley-car manufacturers wanted the speed of telephone talk not to exceed the average speed of the trolley car, or else (they argued) there would be no need to travel to discuss family problems. But the ATT-IBM-GTE-RCA-ITT boys argued smoothly that the national defense required that communications be as swift as the speed of light, although as a sop to the Trolley Lobby they agreed to reduce that speed from infinity to only 186,281 miles per second. The Trolley Lobby's rejoinder, that one country's national defense was another's threat, was never heard above the bleeps and busy signals.

As a forerunner of future differences, labor and management disagreed on the length of the working day. The unions wanted it short; industry, citing computer projections, argued that a long day was the only protection against a weakened dollar and an adverse balance of payments. Finally, a brilliant compromise was reached: the planet earth would be spun forever so that exactly one-half the time would be day and one-half night. The only issue still unresolved is a pending petition by some Hebrews that it be spun the other way.

The only other Law of Nature we'll discuss here is how the Great Sanhedrin dealt with vague witnesses who, as they testified about the earth's problems, drifted further and further off; several wandered off to Pluto and beyond. Things got to be so light-headed, so tentative, that the banks were charging floating interest rates. It was agreed that things had to be pinned down or all would be lost somewhere in outer space, hence quick passage of the Law of Gravity.

Having completed its assignment, or most of it, the Great Sanhedrin adjourned sine die. Its laws aren't perfect (for instance, the Law of Gravity has made some people fall), but by and large they work creditably well. The point is that even where they don't work, people over the ages have learned to adjust; for instance, football players wear shoulder pads and helmets. But there is a stirring now that New York City can't adjust to the drought, and for the first time in twenty-one eons there is a suggestion that the Great Sanhedrin should be reconvened.

Some of the city's scientists have proposed that the Laws of Nature be amended so that rain will not be the only source of water; perhaps (these scientists say) idle talk and foolish ideas could be converted into water at the option of the hearer (according to a formula to be worked out by the Sanhedrin's subcommittee on weights and measures). If so, the City Council's attempt to amend the law mandating where orange ices can, and can't, be sold would be transmuted into enough water not only to fill the city's reservoirs forever but to make the Sahara bloom.

September 5, 1985

In the Name of the Law

Attorney General Edwin Meese 3d has started a furor by asserting that only the named parties were bound by Supreme Court decisions. But, as usual, the attorney general is on the cutting edge of jurisprudence; and, as usual, his critics have been so quick to holler that they have missed the point.

What the attorney general has done, in the laissez-faire spirit of this administration, is to offer the American people choices they never enjoyed before. For instance, under the Meese Doctrine, any little black girl who wants to attend a desegregated public school may do so; the only requirement is that her father change his name to Oliver Brown (the Brown in *Brown v. Board of Education of Topeka, Kansas*). And so, by the flick of a legal switch, as if by magic, any American can succeed to all the rights of any named litigant who ever lived.

If a person expects to be arrested in the forthcoming year or two but doesn't want to blurt out a confession before the arrival of his attorney, he could, by shrewdly anticipating his problem, change his name in advance to Ernesto A. Miranda. That, by the way, would doubtless lead to greater police efficiency, which is probably exactly what the wise old A.G. had in mind. The point is that a detective would be secretly assigned to tail each such name-changer, and so would be an actual witness to the heinous crime. No longer would the police have to rely on vague, circumstantial evidence. On the other hand, a girl who changed her name to Jane Roe (as in *Roe v. Wade*) would, to the dismay of her parents and clergyman, be giving her boyfriend a clue as to her availability.

Many children of accountants would be named Irs, which is not a misspelling of Iris, a Greek mythological character; few accountants steep themselves in the classics. The name is, rather, the acronym for the Internal Revenue Service, which was the named party in many Supreme Court cases that upheld tax loopholes and quick write-offs.

The elegant Ivy League law firms, with their expertise in Supreme Court litigation, sought to limit the attorney general's principle to that one Court, where they would have their intellectual monopoly. But other, lesser practitioners, with the inexorable logic of precedent, argued that the new wondrous idea should be followed by all the courts in the land. And soon over one billion cases representing all the reported litigation from every state, county, and hamlet in America (from 1776 to date) were being processed so that every citizen, from the Atlantic to the Pacific, could be given the fullest range of "named parties" and their awful deeds from which to select. The process was a great boon to the ailing computer industry, for all the high-tech machines produced by IBM and Japan together could still not keep up with the demand. Memory chips that had been adequate for both Star Wars and baseball statistics were soon hopelessly outdated.

Although the attorney general was proud of his free-enterprise Jurisprudential Revolution (there was nothing like it in any of the wishy-washy administrations past) some results were, to be candid, lackluster. For one, any citizen could murder (or rob) any other with impunity because all that was needed for a complete defense was the adoption of the name of any reported murderer (or robber) who had beaten the rap. Most lawyers, with their trusty computers (some of which were larger than the Empire State Building) could come up with dozens of such names in a nanosecond. The advantage of that choice was that one didn't have to change one's ethnicity in order to escape jail.

The chaos was not only on the streets. As millions of Americans changed their names every month, the Postal Service and telephone directory compilers fell further and further behind. The nation became so atomized that our motto was reversed to E Unum Pluribus. Cartographers labeled the lower forty-eight as the Anarchic States of America. Finally, even Edwin Meese 3d began to realize that his favorite new principle, although brilliant, did not reflect the original intent of the Founding Fathers, which was "to form a more perfect Union."

November 17, 1986

Gramm-Rudman and Serendipity

The Administration Office of the United States Courts listed the budget cuts that it was making in order to comply with Congress's new law, the Deficit Reduction Act, popularly known as Gramm-Rudman. Among those budget cuts was this item: spending for law books would be curtailed or even terminated. This essay reflects on those cuts.

When the spirit of the devil was infused into them, the swine ran into the sea and drowned; so it is recounted in Matthew 8:28–30. The contemporary equivalent of those demons is the Deficit Reduction Act, known as Gramm-Rudman; it, too, brings on instantaneous self-destruction. Such a total, drastic effect is baffling to demonologists, because that congressional mandate requires only a modest 5 percent reduction in expenses. The lesson is that when bureaucrats want to self-destruct or, more to the point, when they want to threaten self-destruction, they can out-finesse, out-bluff the most cloven-footed of devils.

Thus, the navy could comply with the new budget requirements by building nineteen of the twenty dreadnoughts now on the drawing board. But the admirals, to prove the law's unworkability, have decided instead to build all twenty battle-wagons, but all slightly incomplete; each will have a small, hardly noticeable, 5 percent aperture far below the Plimsoll mark, at the very bottom. Budget restrictions, protest the Joint Chiefs, are threatening our national security. Rather than see the whole flotilla sink, Congress has rescinded any Pentagon cuts.

Likewise, the reaction of the Department of Transportation. It could build "only" ninety-five of each of the one hundred highways scheduled for construction and no one would ever know the difference. But it has chosen to build all one hundred, leaving them each "only" 5 percent short of connecting. Hence, all bridges almost make it to the other side, resulting in delays. The back-up was 143 miles, stretching to the Rhode Island border, because one of the westbound lanes of the George Washington Bridge didn't quite reach New Jersey; use of the Lincoln or Holland Tunnels was recommended. Under the gridlock pressure, the cuts were restored.

What prompts this essay is the recent announcement by the Administrative Office of the United States Courts in Washington of how the federal judiciary will handle its Gramm-Rudman reductions. Getting into the sabre-rattling spirit, the law has issued the gravest threat of all: the courts will buy no more law books. To the administrator's surprise, there has been no public outcry, not a whimper. To most citizens, law books are merely a prop, a brown buckram background against which all judges prefer to be photographed. Therefore, there is no reason why the several hundred thousand law books already in stock won't do just fine.

But to lawyers the threat is intriguing: what would happen if, indeed, there *were* no more law books? I myself can think of no harm but of many benefits. It would mean, for instance, that no new laws could be enacted and that there could be no more interpretations of the old ones. The law would be frozen exactly where it is now. That would be the first time in history that *that* has ever happened, and if nothing else, it would be worth the experiment. Unlike physics or biology or sports (where world records are always being broken), the law doesn't make "progress."

There is no reason to believe that the law at this instant is any better or worse than it was a thousand law books back or than it will be a thousand (or a millon) law books hence. Indeed, to some scholars the law was at its best when John Marshall was chief justice; they would discard all law books published after 1835 (the year of his retirement). That would save everybody a lot of library space. Others (but not many outside of his immediate descendants) prefer Justice Waite. And still others will choose Hughes or Warren or Taft or Taney. And, if I read the public mood correctly, many will favor the current Court. A strong argument can be made that the law ought not be frozen without benefiting from the influence of at least one woman jurist.

No new laws will mean no more lobbyists, and what a blessing that will be. A hundred years from now, when political scientists study the sudden, amazing disappearance in 1986 of all those special interest pleaders, they will find it hard to believe that it was the serendipitous result of Gramm-Rudman, of allocating more money to the navy to keep it afloat. It will be hard for anyone to believe all that, but it happened just that way, and that's the gospel.

May 20, 1986

The Lament of the Single Practitioner

IX. *Public Scandals*

Sisyphus and Ivan Boesky

Although they never tapped his telephones—the Greeks prized privacy more than we—Sisyphus was the first man apprehended for having violated the federal securities laws. Homer described him as "fraudulent and avaricious." For punishment, Sis (as the Athenian tabloids soon called him) was dispatched to the Lower World, where he had to roll "a monstrous stone" up a hill forever, for it always rolled down just as it was about to reach the summit. It was said that to the Greeks no punishment could be worse because they abhorred a Means without an End.

On the other hand, Ivan Boesky, our modern-day Sisyphus, has enjoyed to the hilt his Means without End. So it may be harder to fashion a meaningful punishment for him. What the SEC has done, requiring him to pay a $50 million fine on top of his $50 million repayment, is nothing other than the typical, unimaginative, mechanical application of the Old Testament's standard—an eye for an eye. Were Boesky sentenced by the same Olympian tribunal that sentenced Old Sis, his punishment would be more subtle and more appropriate.

Despite the ACLU's objections, Boesky would spend his life in Hades eternally, where he would be kept busy but frustrated: every day he would dial each of his three hundred office telephones, and they would ring and ring in informers' offices all over the world, but nobody would ever answer; every day, before the stock market opening, he would receive a whispered tip about a merger that was consummated last year; his only market quotes would be last month's; and every day would be Christmas Day, only because the stock market was closed. Oh, how he would want to give another $50 million or $100 million instead.

Brooding on it all, we note that the stock market scandals of today are just like the scandals of the 1930s, just like Sisyphus's various schemes, for greed seems to be among the most enduring qualities of all. But, sadly, that does not mean that the innocent escape without punishment, for according to some philosophers (see Albert Camus) we are all like Sisyphus, for each of us pushes our own stone uphill every day with the end—if, indeed, there is an end—never achievable. Does that mean, therefore, philosophically, that we are all (whether avaricious or charitable) doomed to suffer the same fate?

Such an interpretation of the parable may mean that only the very young know right from wrong. For only the very young believe that there is a Heaven and a Hell, because only the very young believe in miracles in which the virtuous triumph and the wicked are destroyed. Once you get out into what is euphemistically called the "real world," once you begin to push that large stone relentlessly up the hill, the line between Heaven and Hell begins to blur.

Are Sisyphus and Boesky the norm or the exception? Do they mock us with their riches, or we them because they are punished? Odysseus reports that when he saw Sisyphus in the Lower World "He was suffering strong pains" as he "struggled" with "the monstrous stone" and "sweat ran all down his body" (*The Odyssey*, book 11, lines 593–600, Lattimore translation). It would be nice to think that Boesky is suffering and sweating over his punishment, over his "monstrous stone," but somehow I doubt it. He's still hoping that on his very next try he'll reach the top, that someone, somewhere, will pick up the phone.

December 16, 1986

The Tower Report—A Classical View

Until I reached appendix B, I thought the Tower Commission Report was just another of those long-winded official whitewashes, just about what one would expect from two dour senators and a grim lieutenant general. It was preachy and smug from start to finish ("If but one of the major policy mistakes we examined had been avoided, the nation's history would bear one less scar, one less embarrassment, one less opportunity for opponents to reverse the principles this nation seeks to preserve and advance in the world," page 99 of the New York Times Book version); and it contained nothing that was not already universally known (the arms that were sent to Iran were not shipped from Sears Roebuck, but from Tiffany, and the mark-up was sent to the Contras). The Report, by its very tediousness, seemed to have been bogged down in the very bureaucratic style it sought to criticize.

But dullness was not my main concern, for no one expected a piece by S. J. Perelman. The real problem was that the Report lacked fire, a moral intensity. There was no outrage that junior clerks could involve our nation in wars on two continents.

Then I began to read appendix B, and I suddenly realized that all that wordiness was just a thick cover for a devastating commentary. The appendix begins with the Report's only literary reference, a short quote, in Latin, from Juvenal, Satire 6, line 347: "Quis custodiet ipsos custodes" ("But who will guard the guards").

Those four Latin words are the only meaningful ones in the Report's 550 small-type pages, the only words that make a point. But what a telling point it is. If properly understood, it means that the Tower Commission, subtly, has put the Iran-Contra affair in its broadest and most meaningful social and political context. In Satire 6, the guards (line 347) would be guarding faithless wives who luxuriated in an immoral, amoral society. Since these women bedded with anyone and everyone, they'd surely seduce their guards as well. Rome's unseemly wealth was its undoing, and there was no escape from the wickedness:

> Luxury, deadlier than any armed invader, lies like an incubus
> Upon us still, avenging the world we brought to heel.
> Since Roman poverty perished, no visitation
> Of crime or lust has been spared us.
>
> [Satire 6, lines 291–295,
> from the Penguin Classics translation]

Is not the Tower Commission suggesting, by its pointed reference, that America, like Rome, has gone astray? Isn't it saying, albeit obliquely, that our unprecedented wealth has made us, like Rome, indulgent and arrogant? Isn't it advising us, by its crisp reference to Satire 6, that both Iran and Nicaragua pose moral questions that cannot be resolved by such material things as TOW missiles and hoards of cash?

By citing Juvenal, the commission has given us a deep insight, and a warning. Juvenal wrote in the waning of the Roman Empire; the best, the Golden Ages of Cicero and Augustus, had already passed. Could that be true of us, too? The Tower Report can make one think.

Both the president and his Democratic rivals have endorsed the Report. One wonders if, in the hectic press of state business, they may not have, momentarily, forgotten their Latin studies.

April 7, 1987

A *Vain Gift*

The retiring chairman of the SEC, John S. R. Shad, has donated $30 million to the Harvard Business School to fund a program to improve Wall Street ethics. I've seen those Harvard Business School types in action, and believe me, $30 million won't make a dent. Nevertheless, a good-faith effort must be made to spend that offering wisely and appropriately, and here are several suggested programs:

1. Every freshman entering the Harvard Business School will be given a Bible. Of course, $30 million purchases a lot of King James versions, especially if in paperback, but only one Good Book per future banker is needed. The only practical solution would be to present each incoming student with a Gutenberg Bible. A drawback would be that those books, with their ornate leather bindings, are bulky and do not fit easily into an attaché case, especially if the case is already packed with inside information.

2. Or, the $30 million could be used to build a nondenominational temple, one modeled (of course, since this is Harvard) on the Parthenon. It would be open every day (except when the stock market was open), twenty-four hours a day, for prayer, meditation, and the exchange of cash. There would be beautiful stained-glass representations of famous scenes: of Ivan Boesky on the telephone; of traders sniffing cocaine; and of some very young arbitragers wearing gold stickpins and silver handcuffs. This Parthenon-on-the-Charles would have ninety-two Doric columns, twice the number of columns that support the smaller version on the Acropolis. This Cambridge cenotaph would be dedicated to that legendary ruler of Phrygia, the patron saint of the Harvard Business School, King Midas.

3. Or, the money could fund a lecture series on ethics. With such a goodly sum, this would not be the usual dull academic presentation. Rather this well-endowed sermon would be given in Carnegie Hall and would be beamed by satellite to Harvard Business School alumni in board rooms throughout the galaxies. The

background music, played by the New York Philharmonic, would feature Handel's *Messiah* (believed by many old "B" school grads to have been dedicated to President Herbert Hoover, who rejected socialistic solutions to the Great Depression). It would be hoped that the oratorio's selection from Isaiah 40:4—"the crooked shall be made straight"—means that even those few graduates who have strayed would be cleansed and welcomed back so that they, too, would be able to enjoy the bull market.

If Mr. Shad is correct, and money can purify the professions, why stop at $30 million for tomorrow's investment bankers? For instance, on that scale, a $60 million gift would immunize from any moral deviation all future dentists; and $120 million (make that $240 million) would save the souls of all future clergymen.

But I suspect that Mr. Shad is wrong, and that money isn't the solution to Wall Street's scandals. Money is, rather, the very cause of the rot; it is the idol, the golden calf. When Moses ascended Mount Sinai to receive the Tablets of the Law, the Israelites built golden calves as idols, and offered them sacrifices. But when that Prophet returned, and witnessed the false and hollow worship, he dashed the Tablets to the ground in anger and broke them. That ethical crisis was resolved when the golden calves were destroyed; only then were the Tablets of the Law restored.

That biblical parable does not mean, necessarily, that the Harvard Business School, that most golden of the world's golden calves, should be dismantled; that would be too much to hope for. But it does suggest, if Exodus (chapters 30–34) is still a guide, that Mr. Shad's extravagant sacrifice will be in vain.

May 6, 1987

X. *Parables and Analogies*

A *Not So Cloistered Life*

When they learned that budget cuts (in the National Endowment for the Arts) might close all museums, the culture buffs were dismayed; they held rallies and signed petitions. But most of the Cloister Bestiary were too stoned to comment; they were celebrating Bastille Day, or was it St. Crispin's Day, or the birthday of the curator's brother-in-law. Finally one gargoyle, after his fifth cup of mead, said: "Oh well, we've been chiseled before."

A Fourteenth Century door, never much of a swinger, moaned: "We're in a jamb now."

The curator summed it up: "We could have managed with a frieze, but not with this drastic reduction."

Of materials impervious, the Cloister People had witnessed Man's follies and triumphs for eight centuries. They wondered aloud what kind of society would close museums, the only humidity-controlled keepers of all things past. Their insights were strangely human.

The Unicorn suggested that the cutbacks were all aimed directly at him (hence were discriminatory; get him a lawyer) because all the people really visited the museum just to see him. While the others were rather crudely crafted in alabaster or granite, he was woven with golden thread. Some grotesques, who were only marginally popular, had endured his preening for centuries and finally complained: "You have one horn and you're always blowing it. But you're no Louis Armstrong."

The Basilisk and the Manticore, both of whom had great speed and deception, didn't care if all the museums closed permanently. In expectation of needing new jobs, they had been reading the newspapers; they decided that, with the sounds of their names, they could probably get high-paying positions in the National Football League. So although a little "On Temporary Loan" sign marks their absence, both the Basilisk and the Man- *215* ticore are headed, right now, for the Pittsburgh Steeler training camp.

The Centaur put on his spectacles; being half-man he was prone to speechifying. He read a long paper on inflation and supply-side economics. The museum was closing, he intoned, because everything was too costly. He remembered, wistfully, when he could ride downtown on the A train for a nickel. The Cloister economy, he intoned, had all the wrong priorities. Too much unproductive Capital was being wasted on Doric and Ionic frills, and not enough on suits of armor. But when he warned of the missal buildup at the Morgan Library, even the Pentagon blushed.

Throughout the discussion, the Dragon snorted his snorts of fire. Every time he breathed he violated the Clean Air Act. The Unicorn had once suggested that the Dragon should keep up with the times and buy a catalytic converter, but he (the Dragon) wouldn't even switch to unleaded beef stew.

Still, it was a matter of raising enough money to keep the museum open. The Griffin, the Cloister's most knowledgeable politician, gave this report: what it takes to get federal funding is a successful lobby. He had seen the Fontainebleau in Miami (at a convention of retired Griffins) and assured the Cloister People that their lobby—the Sistine Chapel—was even more beautiful. Those Cloisterers who were sober wondered at the strange ways of American politics.

Then the Siren spoke. She knew a thing or two about being lulled into false security. Government support, she argued, was the essence of false security. She told of how another government supported the Hermitage Museum, and there was not one Russian artist that anyone could name; nor one poet, except in the samizdat press. And think of what happened to Osip Mandelstam. And what if some Commissioner of Culture in Washington decided that an Andy Warhol Can of Tomato Soup could be hung at the Cloisters, just beside a rose window. All groaned except the Dragon, who was always hungry.

The Cloister People had much to think about. Would a reduction in government involvement in the Arts be a monument to a brilliant policy or a caricature of our society? Monument or

Caricature? The same question has been asked for centuries about the Unicorn, the Basilisk, and the Centaur themselves. And about each of the rest of us.

August 6, 1981

*Parables
and
Analogies*

Strike Four

For most of our history, federal judges remained in office for life, that is, until they retired or died. But a few years ago, attracted by the high salaries, several federal judges left the bench to join prosperous law firms. This essay suggests that it is wrong for federal judges to act like baseball players playing out their options.

Federal judges have been so busy recently issuing injunctions and weighing offers from prosperous law firms that they have not had time to toast their patron, Gouverneur Morris, a delegate to the Constitutional Convention from Pennsylvania.

The original draft of the Constitution prohibited any decrease or increase in a judge's salary: "To hold their offices during good behavior and to receive fixed salaries in which no increase or diminution shall be made so as to affect the persons at the time in office."

Mr. Morris proposed that salary increases, but not decreases, should be allowed on the omniscient ground of possible future inflation; and Benjamin Franklin seconded the motion. But James Madison, a delegate from Virginia, strongly disagreed. He argued that the principle of separation of powers meant that no member of the judiciary should ever be beholden to the legislature; therefore, he reasoned, judicial salaries had to be permanent and fixed. He suggested that the potential problem of inflation could be solved by pegging salaries to the price of wheat. Mr. Morris's motion was passed, six states voting aye, two states voting no, and the others not recorded. (See Debates of July 18, 1787; recorded in *Notes of the Debate in the Federal Convention of 1787 Reported by James Madison*, Ohio University Press, 1966, pp. 317–18.)

Some historians believe that if Madison had been successful in freezing the salaries of some government officials he would have won a really high place in American history, rather than being known only as the man who drafted our Constitution.

But Messrs. Morris and Franklin could not have foreseen that federal judges would feel free to seek their own pay raises by playing out their options, like Catfish Hunter and Tommy John, and signing up with the highest bidder. It is a very sensitive subject to write about, especially for me, because how I miss that Tommy John. Every year, when the final standings are published, I deduct John's won-and-lost record from the Yankees (where he never should have been) and add it to the Dodgers (he never should have left). That's why I don't follow the World Series, because only I know that the real pennant winners aren't playing.

If federal judges want to take advantage of the favorable contract negotiated by the Major League Players Association, they should also be required to undertake the ballplayers' risks. As the legal boys put it, you can never get the benefits of a contract without assuming the burdens (*cum onere*). When a ballplayer muffs a few, it's down to the Three-I League; and it does not matter how many United States senators he knows. Would those federal judges who are always being reversed be willing to be sent down to some municipal court? They would probably cite the Constitution, which grants lifetime tenure to federal judges, as if that clause wasn't meant, primarily, to protect the People.

A merger of the baseball and federal court rules was not easy. Judges, who regularly enforce the one-man, one-vote concept, were appalled to learn that it took only three pitches to strike a batter out but four pitches to walk him. Baseball, fearing that it had been acting unconstitutionally, agreed to the change, although it meant a lot of revisions in the record book. For instance, George Herman Ruth struck out 1,330 times over twenty-two seasons (he hit a total of 714 home runs); with a fourth strike required he might not have struck out at all. The record book is going to have a lot of asterisks.

Another problem was the appeal play. When a runner tags up from third, and an appeal is made that he left the bag too soon, that appeal is decided in about two seconds. If the defensive team will now be required to file a printed record and brief (see Rule 10 of the Rules of Appellate Procedure) some fans would have to leave before the game is over, for who could sit there and live on lukewarm franks for six years? Those who prefer jai-alai and claim that baseball is too slow would have another argument.

Although baseball men were willing to accept a lot of procedural changes in order to merge the federal court system into baseball, they absolutely refused to accept a new rule, proposed by the judges, that would permit a person to be an umpire one year and a player the next. It was hard to articulate their opposition, especially when the judicial representatives were so eloquent in favor of the clause. "Under the Fourteenth Amendment to the Constitution," intoned one Harvard Law School type, "every person, even a judge, is entitled to do whatever task his ability and destiny may decree (citing cases)."

A utility outfielder (hitting .278) responded: "Umpires make hard decisions every day, and those decisions are binding forever. If a runner is called out at the plate, that's how it goes into the record book, even if a video-replay shows that the tag was missed. The game couldn't be played if decisions could be changed even five minutes later. Nobody makes a man become an umpire, but if he makes that decision he should be bound to it forever, the way we are bound by his decisions forever."

That surprisingly emotional speech convinced the ballplayers that a merger between baseball and the federal courts was unworkable. They refused to merge with a group that did not know the difference between an umpire and a player and, even more strangely, that kept some of its very best people on the bench. The fans agreed.

If a baseball player can change his job for higher pay, why not a federal judge? Perhaps because no ballplayer has lifetime tenure (for who would pay $1.20—or was that long ago—to see a seventy-year-old pitcher try to fool a seventy-year-old batter?). And perhaps, too, because Benjamin Franklin, James Madison, Gouverneur Morris, George Washington, and other delegates to the Constitutional Convention would not have cared whether or not there was an Independent Baseball but cared so much they fought a Revolution for an Independent Judiciary.

March 30, 1981

The Laws of Heaven and Earth

Boll weevil or drought, every year our legislatures produce a bumper crop of new laws. One would suppose that by now every conceivable law would have been passed, but those great deliberative bodies—the senates, city councils, boards, bureaus, and commissions—keep finding new ways to govern, hence to improve, our lives. Most of these new laws are just so much alfalfa; and there are so many bushels of them that there is no longer a place to store them. Libraries, overflowing with statutes and regulations, have turned the excess over to stately archives; and the archives store them in humidity-controlled warehouses hoping they'll keep. But laws are like musical instruments; if they are not used they become flat. And most laws are not used because they cannot even be read, because one of those very regulations has closed all the libraries.

Some economists have suggested that we use our surplus laws for barter, giving, for instance, the Saudis two antitrust statutes and a used criminal code (the one without capital punishment) in exchange for a year's supply of low-sulphur oil. The Saudis are, however, hard bargainers; they might want, in addition, a few years' worth of precedents to give their area stability. With a few young lawyers, and a lobbyist, the Saudis could probably produce their own unneeded laws; but with the present cost of lawyers, even the Saudis admit that hiring more than one or two would be a strain.

Most legislators are lawyers who are not even bright enough to be judges; yet they think they have the obligation to tinker, tinker, tinker with our lives. Lawmakers (the very title inflates their souls) firmly believe that passing laws, passing laws, passing laws is the key to salvation. And so, in New York State, for instance, you have to pick up after your dog every day, but you can't buy beer on Sunday.

Having regulated every single one of Man's (and dog's) activities, the legislators are now free, at long last, to turn their attention to the obsolete Laws of Nature. Several school boards have decreed that the Creation took place 5,500 years ago; thus, by a simple majority vote a few fundamentalists, who don't know the difference between the Brontosaurus and the Bronte Sisters, have neatly solved the perplexing problem of why the dinosaurs disappeared.

Seeing how easy it was to amend the Laws of Nature, peace groups campaigned to repeal the Law of Gravity. For if there were no gravity, no bombs could fall, and missiles, aimed at some population center, would just continue harmlessly off into space. On that basis, the New York City Council, eager to beat out Berkeley, California, for the Nobel Prize, voted overwhelmingly to annul the Law of Gravity. But an unforeseen hitch developed when the Politburo in Moscow, after a heated debate, voted unanimously not to do likewise. So while wars continued to rage, New York City had a drought because no rain could fall.

When the issue was debated in the United Nations, the Australian delegate was called a warmonger when he suggested that without gravity his countrymen would simply fall off the globe; they were, he noted, perched rather precariously on the underside as it was. But the secretary general stated, quite correctly, that no vote could satisfy everyone. Whereupon a group of Concerned Physicists, left over from the nuclear energy days, submitted a technical paper to the effect that, without gravity, all the planets would stray from their paths and lose the warmth of the sun. But the General Assembly, voting with its accustomed blocs, discarded that warning as mere orbiter dicta. Unless there is a veto, there will be a lot of changes in the way we live.

But Gravity wasn't the only law to be challenged. Closer to home, the Long Island Railroad was offended by Einstein's arbitrary rule that nothing could exceed the speed of light. The railroad petitioned the Interstate Commerce Commission to exempt its Port Washington Express from what it claimed was an outmoded and onerous limitation; the LIRR claimed that its new, expensive diesels were forced to operate at only half-throttle so as not to violate the unwarranted law of physics. The commission, in the spirit of deregulation, ruled that nothing in Nassau or Suffolk counties—including, specifically, light—could exceed the speed of the railroad's new locomotives. That is why people on The Island have to turn on their lamps about ten minutes before they begin to read.

A group of worrywarts and editorial writers voiced concern that legislative changes were getting out of hand. They suggested that since the Laws of Nature had been unchanged for twenty billion years, it was egotistical of Man (who has only been able to read for a few thousand years) to meddle. But Einstein's laws are less than a hundred years old, and, nevertheless, scientists consider them to be binding; as, indeed, scientists had once considered Newton's laws (now obsolete) to be binding.

Can it be that the laws that govern the Heavens, and hold in place millions of galaxies and billions of stars, are as fleeting and as whimsical as the laws that govern on Earth?

April 28, 1981

The Law from Yavapai Point

The Grand Canyon of the Colorado, the most awesome void in the world except for the Theory of Supply-Side Economics, is 217 miles long, 10 miles wide, and 1 mile deep. This is an essay of some rambling summer observations from Yavapai Point about the canyon and the law.

The canyon was carved without debate and without any cost to the taxpayer. Had the Congress undertaken the same task, it might have taken longer than the two billion years it took Nature. Some Democrats, poring over the blueprints, would protest that the canyon was, at least as planned, much too small. On the other side, Secretary of Interior James Watt would testify that since Washington, D.C., already had a subway system, another large government-owned hole-in-the-ground was not warranted.

Further delay would be caused by the litigation over the Environmental Impact Statement. Since claims are usually lodged on behalf of all affected species, there would be separate amicus briefs filed on behalf of the birds, the squirrels, and the bighorn sheep, because their lives would be dramatically changed. For instance, for reasons not clearly understood, only larger birds (ravens, hawks, and eagles) routinely fly from rim to rim. Smaller birds (which can fly hundreds of miles over flat surfaces), simply refuse to fly over the canyon, but tediously go down one side and up the other. The bluebirds' special counsel would note that the trip would add many unnecessary stops and hours to each small bird's journey: "You'll not make another Conrail of us" he proclaimed, filing an official protest with the ICC. And over at the FTC the staff would be all aflutter for years, pondering the antitrust implications of favoring large birds over small.

The squirrels would have an even stronger argument. They would be unable to cross the canyon floor at all, and so their lives would be forever limited to one side of the river or the other. That might violate some inalienable right under the Helsinki Treaty, or so some court could well decide. If the canyon were to be built,

it would cause the employment of three lawyers and two paralegals for every digger.

The canyon puts things in perspective. For instance, it's nice to
think (especially after losing an appeal) that the thirty-story United
States Courthouse, which so aristocratically dominates Foley
Square, could fit into one niche, one burrow of the Grand Canyon, and be hidden forever. Would federal judges issue fewer injunctions and mandamuses if they presided in a less imperial
building, one without a golden roof? And if the whole building
were to disappear into the canyon's vastness, would one of those
eager archaeologists in a Brooks Brothers pith helmet discover it
thousands of years hence and wonder why so large a courthouse
was needed in an area thought to be inhabited only by a small
tribe of nonlitigious Havasupai Indians?

If a whole courthouse could be hidden, why not find a crevice
for my own office and papers. I could then stay at the canyon
forever, photographing sunset and dawn every day, and never
worry about delays on the A train or a briefing schedule. And if
someone were to chance on the spot a million years from now, let
him try to bring some order to my filing system. I'd be grateful for
any help. Perhaps, too, he'll file normal substitution papers and
answer the interrogatories; the responses were due a few days
after my return, but adjournments are routinely granted.

The rapids are ferocious. What a place to drop some precedents
that one would like undone. In an instant they'd disintegrate and
become part of the silt that lines the river bank. Each level of rock
in the canyon tells a story of time past. Embedded in the rock are
jellyfish imprints from the Proterozoic era (620 million years
ago), shell fragments from the Paleozoic era (only 230 million
years ago), and fossils from animals long extinct. Perhaps some
legal scholar, while hiking on Bright Angel Trail a long, long time
from now, will recognize fragments from *Gregg v. Georgia* (the
case upholding capital punishment) or *Eisen v. Carlisle & Jac-
quelin* (a case I lost in the Supreme Court 9–0) and wonder why
those holdings did not survive, except as shards.

Judges meander. Some leave the bench to join monied law
firms; some to run for political office. Some others, many others,

impose their own personal preferences on the law. Still others, many others, decide cases on tangential grounds, never resolving the issues before them. Perhaps instead of going to judicial conferences all members of the judiciary should be taken once each year to the Grand Canyon to observe how one river that stayed its narrow course faithfully has done more to shape our country than all the judges since John Jay.

October 16, 1981

A *Material Improvement in Criminal Law*

The New York State Legislature, pressed to end violent crime, has made it a separate felony to wear a bullet-proof vest while illegally using a firearm. If the purpose of this state-enforced dress code is to curb outlaws, we suggest that it is too narrow, too tight-fitting. For instance, the legislatures could end all wintertime robberies forthwith in places like Buffalo, Chicago, and Sioux Falls by making it illegal, while en route to a hold-up, to wear ear muffs. London, England, and Portland, Oregon, could protect their banks and citizens by passing a similar edict against wearing raincoats; likewise, boots and/or bolo ties in Texas and false teeth in Miami Beach. Finally, one wise state senate, over the objections of the haberdashers' lobby, could aggregate all the wisdom and make it a separate offense to wear any clothing during the commission of a burglary. The result would fascinate criminologists: there would surely be a dramatic decrease in thefts committed by skinny men and fat women.

Congress, seeing how easy it was to end all tax evasion, could make it illegal for accountants to wear white collars.

Had the fine points of sartorial law been understood earlier, history might have been changed. For instance, the Roman Senate could have made it a separate wrong, effective as of 12:01 A.M. on March 15, 44 B.C., for anyone to stab a government official while wearing a toga.

But we do not mean to disparage the New York Legislature for its ban on bullet-proof vests because the law will furnish work for attorneys and tailors for years to come. In particular, the law defines the banned vest as one which contains "at least seven layers of bullet-resistant material" which would stop a .38 caliber bullet going at 850 feet per second. The boys on Seventh Avenue, when properly motivated, could easily fashion a mere six-layer vest, each layer carefully stuffed like a Reuben sandwich, that could stop a cannon shell. Those legal six-packs would come in a variety of shades and designs to match the season; I understand that a brown herringbone heads the spring line. According to the instructions on the label, it should be dry-cleaned whenever the wearer launders his money.

The above is but a prologue to a serious discussion of the significant relationship between law and fabric: Why do judges wear black robes? Is it a symbol of the law's bleakness and lack of humor? Are judges merely copying those among the clergy who consider themselves to have been divinely appointed? Is it just a uniform, like those worn in English schools, so that all magistrates, rich and poor, will look alike? Is it a cloak of authority, like military khaki or the policeman's blue? The fact is that the black robe represents none of those pretentious things. Judges don't like to admit it, but the first judge's wife chose the black robe because she wanted him to wear something practical, something that he could don day in and day out without showing the dirt. From that humble beginning, a large mystique has grown.

The convicted brigand appeared for sentencing and was asked why he had worn a bullet-proof vest during the heist. He replied: "Your Honor, I had the sniffles, and the doc said to drink plenty of juices and to dress warmly."

The court added three years to his sentence. It proved, said the defendant, that the man in the imperious black had no sense of humor.

It also proved, boasted the Establishment bar, that judges are not sympathetic to the vested interests.

April 27, 1984

A *Law Library Parable*

recent article in the *New York Times* (September 21, 1984, page D20) quoted Mr. Justice Harry Blackmun as having observed that the Supreme Court was "moving to the right." The item was not on page A1, where the *Times* prints its late-breaking bulletins, since Chief Justice Burger had been sworn in to replace Chief Justice Warren in 1969.

What does it mean, that the Court is "moving to the right"? Are there workmen in hard-hats actually digging about the building's foundations, trying to nudge it eastward? Will Washington, D.C., wake up one bright morning to a traffic jam because the Supreme Court itself was blocking the left lane of East Capitol Street?

The more prevalent scholarly view is that the justice was speaking not structurally or architecturally but metaphysically and metaphorically; that his reference was not to the movement of the neo-classical Greek temple that houses the High Court but to the movement of the law.

But if that is so, what does *that* mean? The law is made up of federal, state, county, and local constitutions, statutes, codes, regulations, commentaries, and interpretive decisions, all bound into several hundred thousand volumes and squeezed into library shelves. Does it mean that at a prearranged signal, perhaps at midnight under a full moon, all the law librarians in the nation will simultaneously move all the books a stipulated number of notches rightward? One problem is that all the volumes should probably not be moved the same distance in the same direction. For instance, while the decisions of the federal courts might properly and fairly be reshelved to the right, the opinions of other jurisdictions (Massachusetts, perhaps; it voted for McGovern) should probably stay in place. As a further complication, a few volumes (the ordinances of San Francisco perhaps, with its protection of gay rights) should probably be shifted slightly leftward.

A difficulty even greater than the reshelving of anonymous decisions and statutes, was where to place many of the law texts written by learned authors, often renowned professors at great universities. There were, for instance, treatises on jurisprudence which explained, often in several languages, that the law was objective and fixed, and not, like the tides of public opinion, subject to sudden shifts to the left or right. These academicians even had a motto for their abstract view: "Ours is a government of laws, not of men." That meant, most people thought, that although the popular mood might change, the law would be an ever-steady guide, a North star. If those texts were not moved, there was the fear that they would be overwhelmed by the sudden avalanche of hundreds of thousands of rightward-moving books that had been shelved next to them.

The political science treatises were another particular worry. Several of them contained learned analyses of the system of checks and balances that had made our Constitution the glory of the free world. Those books explained that while the executive and legislative branches might succumb to popular passions, our freedoms were eversafe because the judicial branch, with its historic commitment to eternal principles and time-honored precedents, would never waver. Some librarians suggested that those books, too, should be withdrawn before they were engulfed by the rightward tide, and perhaps stored in the basement along with the 1942 Tax Code and other obsolete matter. Law librarians do get maudlin sometimes.

But what worried the librarians most of all were the very old books, the ones with the fragile bindings and fragile pages. For instance, the Constitution was written in 1787. Could such a venerable book, now almost two hundred years old, stay in place and survive amid the mighty clamor and turbulence on the shelves?

October 15, 1984

Pennzoil-Texaco Case—A Classical View

This essay is about one of the largest corporate mergers in history, Texaco Oil's merger with Getty Oil. Although these billion-dollar fusions are usually handled smooth as silk, this one developed a leak. A third corporate giant, Pennzoil, claimed that it had merged with Getty before Texaco had. As proof of that prior agreement, Pennzoil described how its directors and Getty's had toasted their merger with a late-night champagne party in a fashionable New York hotel. But Texaco claimed that the Pennzoil-Getty agreement had never been made final, so that it (Texaco) was still free to merge with Getty, which it did later that very same night, albeit in a different hotel. When Texaco walked off with Getty, Pennzoil sued. A Houston jury agreed with Pennzoil and socked Texaco with damages of $10.5 billion, by far the largest judgment award in a civil case in the history of the world. This essay puts those events into a classical context.

Paris, son of Priam, wooed fair Helen, Menelaos's wife. Thus began the sad events that led to ten years of war; to the death of Hektor, breaker of horses; to the death of godlike Achilles; and to the sacking of once-mighty Troy. It was, until now, the most star-crossed courtship in history. This essay is about that current lovers' quarrel, the one that pales the events recounted in *The Iliad*; this essay is about the wooing of most fair Gettyoileis, if fair be measured by reserves of crude oil still untapped.

The story begins with Pennzoilos, an ambitious lad of humble birth. Some say he was born in Oklahoma, near Tulsa, and some say it was in Texas, in the Panhandle. All agree that his parents were no better than wandering wildcatters. The young Pennzoilos was unusually diligent, and day and night he drilled and drilled. Soon he owned many wells of oil and many derricks, and he lived in a great mansion in far-off Houston, which was at the very edge of civilization, beyond even where the brave Agamemnon had ever sailed. Despite his burgeoning wealth and growing fame

Pennzoilos was restless, for he longed for even greater wealth and for social respectability. But the richer he became, the more he was ostracized for his less than noble ancestry. Then one day his daring and persistence caught the favorable eye of Pallas Athena, Zeus's sister who lived on Mount Olympus, and she determined to marry him to a princess of oildom's most distinguished and ancient family.

At the very same time, the very same idea occurred to Lazard Freres, a New York investment banking firm that specialized in elegant mergers. And so, with these two very formidable blessings, Pennzoilos was introduced to the most fair Gettyoileis, if fair be measured by reserves of crude oil still untapped. Glances, and then balance sheets, were exchanged, and it was love at first sight.

And oh what a passion it was. It was champagne and nectar in New York's swellest eateries; it was two on the aisle for every sock and buskin on Broadway; it was gifts of monogrammed silver greaves from Cartier (for him) and brocaded off-shoulder togas from Yves St. Laurent (for her). And then to the bridal suite.

In the rosy-fingered dawn, when Pennzoilos awoke, he was startled to find that his Gettyoileis was gone. Shock turned to disbelief and then to bitter anger when he read in the morning newspaper's society column that Gettyoileis, his own fair Gettyoileis, had married Texacos that very night. Texacos was one of oildom's older, portlier, richer princes. From his picture it was clear that he was no Adonis, but he was of noble birth. His father was a large landowner from Peloponnesus and his mother was said to be Eris, goddess of discord.

Distraught, Pennzoilos returned to Houston, which was at the very fringe of the civilized world, where even the brave Agamemnon had never ventured. Every day, as he read more and more about his once beloved Gettyoileis and the portly, smug Texacos and their gushing romance and their partying, he grew angrier and more bitter. Finally, when he saw a picture of her strutting to the opera in one of those brocaded off-shoulder togas for which he himself had paid thousands of drachmas, he could no longer contain himself. He hired a learned lawyer, who advised that it was the clearest case of alienation of affection since Paris visited

Sparta in about 1200 B.C. and stole fair Helen, old Menelaos's wife.

The jury trial in Houston was not only reported throughout the world but was carefully monitored by a furious Pallas Athena, Zeus's sister who dwelled on Mount Olympus, for it was she who had arranged the match between ardent Pennzoilos and fair Gettyoileis, if fair be measured by barrels of oil in the ground. And so Athena sent her furies to Houston, even though Houston was at the far rim of the known world. And the furies worked their sorcery. Texacos, when he testified before the jury, was made to appear even portlier, even more lecherous, as he twisted a large shiny golden pinky ring, a ring that he had never seen before but that had been magically placed on his finger in the midst of his cross-examination. And Pennzoilos, the poor orphan Pennzoilos, appeared to be bereft, although he owned vast stretches of land beyond Macedonia. The jury listened intently as Pennzoilos's lawyer showed charts that had been prepared by Euclid and explained the damage figures as calculated by Pythagoras. And at the end, as Athena laughed, Zeus hurled a thunderbolt to Houston, and the jury awarded 10.5 billion drachmas to Pennzoilos.

Such was the burial of Texacos, breaker of contracts.

January 6, 1986